2024 Edition

The KIDNEY Dialysis COOKBOOK

Full color images

Dr. Keshawn Nicolas

Delicious and Easy Recipes with Preparation Times, Nutritional Values, Meal Plan and Health Benefits

28-DAY Meal Plan

Disclaimer

The information in this cookbook is provided for general informational purposes only and is not intended as medical or nutritional advice. The recipes and meal plans are designed to support kidney health, but individual dietary needs and restrictions may vary. Always consult with a healthcare provider or a registered dietitian before making any significant changes to your diet, especially if you have a medical condition or are undergoing treatment.

The author and publisher are not responsible for any adverse effects or consequences resulting from the use or application of the information contained in this book. The reader assumes all risks and responsibilities associated with the use of the recipes and meal plans provided.

Table of Contents

Introduction

Welcome to ***The Kidney Dialysis Cookbook 2024.*** This book is designed to support those undergoing kidney dialysis by providing a selection of delicious and nutritious recipes that cater specifically to their dietary needs. Navigating the world of kidney dialysis can be challenging, especially when it comes to managing your diet. This introduction will help you understand the essential aspects of kidney dialysis, the crucial role diet plays in this process, and how to make the most out of the recipes in this book.

Understanding Kidney Dialysis

Kidney dialysis is a medical treatment used to perform the essential functions of the kidneys when they are no longer able to do so effectively on their own. The kidneys are essential organs that filter waste materials and excess fluids from the blood, keep electrolytes balanced, and regulate blood pressure. When kidneys fail, dialysis takes over these critical functions.

There are two main types of dialysis:

- **Hemodialysis:** This method uses a machine to filter the blood. A needle is inserted into a blood vessel, and blood is drawn into the machine, cleaned, and then returned to the body. This process is typically done in a dialysis center or, in some cases, at home.
- **Peritoneal Dialysis:** This technique involves inserting a catheter into the abdominal cavity. A special fluid is infused into the cavity to absorb waste products from the blood. After a period of time, the fluid is drained out and replaced with fresh fluid. This can be done manually or with the aid of a machine.

Both types of dialysis require patients to adhere to specific dietary guidelines to help manage their health and ensure the effectiveness of the treatment.

The Importance of Diet in Dialysis

Diet plays a pivotal role in the management of kidney dialysis. Since dialysis is not a perfect replacement for kidney function, maintaining a well-balanced diet is crucial for managing symptoms, preventing complications, and improving overall well-being.

Key reasons diet is important include:

- **Waste Management:** Dialysis patients need to limit the intake of certain nutrients that are difficult for the body to handle or that can accumulate in the blood. These include potassium, phosphorus, and sodium. A controlled diet helps manage these levels and reduces the risk of complications.
- **Fluid Balance:** Excess fluid can build up in the body when kidneys are not functioning properly. By monitoring fluid intake, patients can help control swelling, high blood pressure, and other related issues.
- **Protein Intake:** Dialysis patients need to consume adequate protein to replace what is lost during the treatment process. However, the type and amount of protein need to be carefully managed to avoid stress on the kidneys.
- **Overall Health:** A balanced diet helps maintain energy levels, supports immune function, and promotes general health, all of which are essential for patients undergoing dialysis.

Key Nutritional Considerations

When managing a diet for kidney dialysis, several nutritional considerations come into play:

- **Potassium:** Elevated potassium levels can lead to heart problems. Foods high in potassium, such as bananas, potatoes, and tomatoes, often need to be limited.
- **Phosphorus:** High phosphorus levels can lead to bone and cardiovascular problems. Foods such as dairy products, nuts, and beans are high in phosphorus and may need to be restricted.
- **Sodium:** Excess sodium can lead to high blood pressure and fluid retention. It is essential to limit salt and high-sodium foods, opting for low-sodium alternatives.
- **Protein:** Dialysis patients need enough protein to support overall health but must choose high-quality sources that do not overly stress the kidneys. Lean meats, fish, and eggs are excellent options.
- **Fluid Intake:** Monitoring fluid intake is crucial to avoid complications like swelling and high blood pressure. A fluid allowance will be determined by your healthcare provider based on your individual needs.
- **Vitamins and Minerals:** Dialysis can affect the absorption

of certain vitamins and minerals. A well-rounded diet can help ensure you receive necessary nutrients, though supplements may be required based on your doctor's advice.

How to Use This Cookbook

This cookbook is crafted to provide you with practical, flavorful, and nutritious recipes that align with the dietary needs of dialysis patients. Here's how to make the most out of it:

- **Understand the Recipes:** Each recipe in this book is designed with your dietary restrictions in mind. Ingredients are chosen to be kidney-friendly while providing variety and taste. Pay attention to portion sizes and ingredient lists to stay within your dietary guidelines.
- **Follow the Meal Plan:** The 28-day meal plan at the end of this book offers a structured approach to meal planning, helping you balance your nutrient intake over the course of a month. Adjust portions and ingredients as needed based on your personal health requirements.
- **Customize Recipes:** Feel free to modify recipes according to your taste preferences and dietary needs. Substitutions can be made for ingredients that fit within your specific dietary restrictions.
- **Consult Your Healthcare Provider:** While this cookbook provides general guidance, always consult your healthcare provider or dietitian before making significant changes to your diet. They may provide you tailored recommendations based on your medical history and current health situation.
- **Enjoy Cooking:** Embrace the process of preparing your meals. Cooking can be both a soothing and gratifying activity. Use this cookbook to explore new recipes, enjoy tasty meals, and support your health journey.

By following the guidelines and using the recipes in this cookbook, you can enjoy a variety of meals that are not only satisfying but also supportive of your health needs. Here's to a healthier, more enjoyable dining experience on your dialysis journey!

1
Breakfasts

1. Scrambled Egg Whites with Spinach

Preparation Time

- **10 minutes**

Cooking Time

- **10 minutes**

Serving Unit

- **2 servings**

Ingredients

- **4 large egg whites** (about 1 cup)
- **1 cup fresh spinach leaves**, chopped
- **1 tablespoon olive oil**
- **1/4 cup onion**, finely chopped
- **1 clove garlic**, minced
- **Salt**, to taste (use a low-sodium alternative or omit)
- **Black pepper**, to taste
- **Optional:** 1 tablespoon low-fat cheese, shredded (e.g., mozzarella or cheddar)

Procedures of Preparation

1. **Prepare Ingredients:**
   - Wash and chop the spinach leaves.
   - Finely chop the onion and mince the garlic.
2. **Heat the Pan:**
   - In a nonstick skillet, heat the olive oil over medium heat.
3. **Cook the Vegetables:**
   - Add the chopped onion to the skillet and sauté for 2-3 minutes until it becomes translucent.
   - Add the minced garlic and simmer for another minute, stirring often to prevent burning.
4. **Add Spinach:**

- Add the chopped spinach to the skillet. Cook, stirring occasionally, for 2-3 minutes until the spinach is wilted and tender.

5. **Scramble Egg Whites:**
   - Pour the egg whites in the skillet with the veggies. Stir gently to combine.
   - Cook over medium heat, stirring occasionally, until the egg whites are fully cooked and scrambled. This should take about 3-4 minutes.
6. **Season:**
   - Season with salt and black pepper to taste. If using cheese, sprinkle it over the scrambled egg whites in the last minute of cooking.
7. **Serve:**
   - Divide the scrambled egg whites with spinach between two plates and serve immediately.

Nutritional Values (Per Serving)

- **Calories:** 110
- **Protein:** 11g
- **Carbohydrates:** 2g
- **Fat:** 7g
- **Sodium:** 150mg (using a pinch of salt)
- **Potassium:** 270mg
- **Phosphorus:** 70mg

Note: Nutritional values are approximate and can vary based on specific ingredient brands and quantities used.

Cooking Tips

- **Use a Non-Stick Pan:** A non-stick skillet makes it easier to cook the egg whites without sticking and helps ensure even cooking.
- **Low-Sodium Alternatives:** If you need to reduce sodium further, consider using a salt substitute or simply omit salt entirely.
- **Flavor Enhancements:** Fresh herbs like chives or parsley can add additional flavor without adding extra sodium or potassium.
- **Avoid Overcooking:** Egg whites cook quickly and can become rubbery if overcooked. Stir gently and remove from heat as soon as they are set.

Health Benefits

- **Low in Potassium:** Egg whites are low in potassium, making them suitable for those on a kidney dialysis diet where potassium intake needs to be monitored.
- **High in Protein:** Egg whites provide a high-quality source of protein, essential for muscle

maintenance and overall body repair.

- **Rich in Vitamins and Minerals:** Spinach is a good source of vitamins A and C, folate, and iron, contributing to overall health while being low in potassium.
- **Heart-Healthy Fats:** Olive oil is a source of healthy fats, which can support cardiovascular health.

2. Quinoa Porridge with Blueberries

Preparation Time

- **10 minutes**

Cooking Time

- **20 minutes**

Serving Unit

- **2 servings**

Ingredients

- **1/2 cup quinoa**
- **1 cup water**
- **1 cup unsweetened almond milk** (or any other low-potassium, low-phosphorus milk alternative)
- **1/2 cup fresh blueberries** (or frozen, thawed)
- **1 tablespoon maple syrup** (optional, for sweetness)
- **1/2 teaspoon vanilla extract**
- **1/2 teaspoon ground cinnamon**
- **Pinch of salt** (optional, use a low-sodium option or omit)

Procedures of Preparation

1. **Rinse the Quinoa:**
   - Place the quinoa in a fine-mesh strainer and rinse with cool water. This helps remove the saponins, which can cause a bitter taste.
2. **Cook the Quinoa:**
   - In a medium saucepan, combine the rinsed quinoa and 1 cup of water. Bring to a boil over a medium to high heat.
   - Reduce the heat to low, cover the saucepan, and let it simmer for about 15 minutes, or until the water is absorbed and the quinoa is tender.
3. **Prepare the Porridge:**

- Add the unsweetened almond milk to the cooked quinoa. Stir to combine and bring the mixture to a gentle simmer over medium heat.
- Cook, stirring occasionally, for about 5 minutes, or until the porridge reaches your desired consistency. If it becomes too thick, you can add a bit more almond milk.

4. **Add Flavorings:**
   - Stir in the vanilla extract, ground cinnamon, and a pinch of salt (if using). Mix well to incorporate the flavors.
5. **Add Blueberries:**
   - Gently fold in the fresh or thawed blueberries. Cook for an additional 2-3 minutes, allowing the blueberries to warm through and release their juices into the porridge.
6. **Sweeten (Optional):**
   - If desired, stir in the maple syrup to add a touch of sweetness. Adjust to taste.
7. **Serve:**
   - Divide the porridge between two bowls. Serve warm and enjoy.

Nutritional Values (Per Serving)

- **Calories:** 210
- **Protein:** 6g
- **Carbohydrates:** 36g
- **Fat:** 5g
- **Sodium:** 180mg (using a pinch of salt)
- **Potassium:** 300mg
- **Phosphorus:** 150mg

Note: Nutritional values are approximate and can vary based on specific ingredient brands and quantities used.

Cooking Tips

- **Rinse Quinoa Thoroughly:** Always rinse quinoa before cooking to avoid any bitter taste from the saponins.
- **Adjust Consistency:** If you prefer a creamier porridge, add more almond milk during the cooking process. For a thicker texture, reduce the amount of milk.
- **Flavor Variations:** Experiment with different spices like nutmeg or cardamom, or add a handful of chopped nuts for extra texture and flavor.
- **Sweetener Alternatives:** If you prefer not to use maple syrup, consider a small amount of honey or a sugar substitute that suits your dietary needs.

Health Benefits

- **High in Protein:** Quinoa is a complete protein, meaning it contains all nine essential amino acids, making it an excellent choice for maintaining muscle mass and overall health.
- **Rich in Antioxidants:** Blueberries are packed with antioxidants, particularly vitamin C and flavonoids, which can help combat oxidative stress and inflammation.
- **Low in Sodium:** By using unsweetened almond milk and controlling the amount of added salt, this porridge is low in sodium, making it suitable for a kidney-friendly diet.
- **Heart-Healthy:** The combination of quinoa and blueberries provides heart-healthy nutrients. Quinoa is a good source of fiber, which supports cardiovascular health, while blueberries have been linked to improved heart function and lower blood pressure.
- **Nutrient-Dense:** This porridge provides essential vitamins and minerals, including magnesium, iron, and folate, which contribute to overall health.

3. Low-Sodium Oatmeal with Almonds

Preparation Time

- **10 minutes**

Cooking Time

- **10 minutes**

Serving Unit

- **2 servings**

Ingredients

- **1 cup old-fashioned rolled oats**
- **2 cups water** (or low-sodium, unsweetened almond milk for extra creaminess)
- **1/4 cup sliced almonds**
- **1 tablespoon honey** (or maple syrup, optional for sweetness)
- **1/2 teaspoon ground cinnamon**
- **1/4 teaspoon vanilla extract**
- **1/2 cup fresh or dried fruit** (such as blueberries, apples, or raisins, optional)
- **Pinch of salt** (optional, use a low-sodium option or omit)

Procedures of Preparation

1. **Prepare Ingredients:**
    - Measure out the rolled oats and sliced almonds.
    - If using fresh fruit, wash and chop it into bite-sized pieces. If using dried fruit, ensure it is unsweetened.
2. **Cook the Oats:**
    - In a medium saucepan, combine the oats and water (or almond milk). Bring to a boil over a medium to high heat.
    - Once boiling, reduce the heat to low and simmer, uncovered, for about 5 minutes, stirring occasionally, until the oats

are tender and the liquid is mostly absorbed.

3. **Add Flavorings:**
   - Stir in the ground cinnamon and vanilla extract. If you are using a pinch of salt, add it at this stage.
   - Continue to cook for another 2 minutes to allow the flavors to meld together.
4. **Incorporate Almonds and Sweetener:**
   - Stir in the sliced almonds and honey (or maple syrup), if using. Cook for an additional 1-2 minutes to toast the almonds lightly and incorporate the sweetener.
5. **Add Fruit (Optional):**
   - If you are adding fruit, gently fold it into the oatmeal now. If using dried fruit, consider adding it earlier to allow it to rehydrate.
6. **Serve:**
   - Divide the oatmeal between two bowls. Serve warm and enjoy.

Nutritional Values (Per Serving)

- **Calories:** 220
- **Protein:** 6g
- **Carbohydrates:** 30g
- **Fat:** 8g
- **Sodium:** 10mg (using a pinch of salt)
- **Potassium:** 300mg
- **Phosphorus:** 130mg

Note: Nutritional values are approximate and can vary based on specific ingredient brands and quantities used.

Cooking Tips

- **Use Rolled Oats:** Old-fashioned rolled oats are preferred for this recipe because they cook quickly and have a better texture compared to steel-cut oats or instant oats.
- **Adjust Consistency:** If you prefer a creamier oatmeal, use almond milk instead of water. Add more liquid if needed to achieve your desired consistency.
- **Toast Almonds:** Lightly toasting the almonds in the pan before adding them to the oatmeal can enhance their flavor and crunch.
- **Control Sweetness:** Adjust the amount of honey or maple syrup to suit your taste preferences and dietary needs. For a lower sugar option, consider using a small amount or omitting it entirely.

Health Benefits

- **Low in Sodium:** This recipe is designed to be low in sodium, making it suitable for those on a kidney-friendly diet. By omitting added salt and using unsweetened almond milk, you can manage your sodium intake effectively.
- **Heart-Healthy Fats:** Sliced almonds provide healthy monounsaturated fats and are a good source of vitamin E, which can help support heart health and reduce inflammation.
- **Rich in Fiber:** Rolled oats are high in soluble fiber, which can help regulate blood sugar levels, improve digestive health, and lower cholesterol levels.
- **Antioxidants:** Cinnamon has antioxidant properties that can help reduce oxidative stress and inflammation. Almonds are also rich in antioxidants that contribute to overall health.
- **Versatile and Nutrient-Dense:** This oatmeal can be customized with various fruits and nuts, providing additional vitamins, minerals, and antioxidants. Choosing fresh or dried fruit adds natural sweetness and extra nutrients without excessive sodium or phosphorus.

4. Greek Yogurt with Fresh Berries

Preparation Time

- **5 minutes**

Cooking Time

- **None**

Serving Unit

- **2 servings**

Ingredients

- **1 cup plain Greek yogurt** (preferably low-fat or non-fat)
- **1/2 cup fresh berries** (such as strawberries, blueberries, raspberries, or a mix)
- **1 tablespoon honey** (optional, for sweetness)
- **1 tablespoon chia seeds** (optional, for added texture and nutrients)
- **1/4 teaspoon vanilla extract** (optional, for extra flavor)
- **1 tablespoon chopped nuts** (such as almonds or walnuts, optional for added crunch)

Procedures of Preparation

1. **Prepare the Berries:**
   - Wash the fresh berries thoroughly under cold water. Pat them dry with a paper towel. If using larger berries like strawberries, hull and slice them into bite-sized pieces.
2. **Prepare the Yogurt:**
   - In a bowl, spoon out 1 cup of plain Greek yogurt.
3. **Mix Ingredients:**
   - If desired, stir in the vanilla extract to the yogurt for extra flavor.
   - If using honey, drizzle it over the yogurt and gently mix to combine.
   - Add the chia seeds to the yogurt if you are using

them. Stir well to ensure they are uniformly distributed.

4. **Add Berries:**
    - Top the yogurt with the prepared fresh berries.
5. **Add Optional Toppings:**
    - Sprinkle chopped nuts over the berries if desired for additional texture and crunch.
6. **Serve:**
    - Divide the yogurt mixture between two bowls. Refrigerate until ready to eat, or serve right away.

Nutritional Values (Per Serving)

- **Calories:** 150
- **Protein:** 10g
- **Carbohydrates:** 20g
- **Fat:** 3g
- **Sodium:** 60mg
- **Potassium:** 280mg
- **Phosphorus:** 150mg

Note: Nutritional values are approximate and can vary based on specific ingredient brands and quantities used.

Cooking Tips

- **Choose Unsweetened Yogurt:** Opt for plain Greek yogurt without added sugars to keep the recipe kidney-friendly and lower in phosphorus.
- **Control Sweetness:** Adjust the amount of honey based on your taste preferences and dietary needs. For a lower sugar option, consider using a sugar substitute or omitting the honey altogether.
- **Chia Seeds:** If adding chia seeds, let the yogurt sit for a few minutes after mixing to allow the seeds to absorb some liquid and expand, adding a pleasant texture to the dish.
- **Mix and Match Berries:** Use a mix of berries for a variety of flavors and nutrients. Blueberries are high in antioxidants, while strawberries provide vitamin C.
- **Make Ahead:** This dish can be prepared ahead of time and stored in the refrigerator for a quick and easy snack or breakfast. However, add fresh berries just before serving to maintain their texture and flavor.

Health Benefits

- **High in Protein:** Greek yogurt is an excellent source of protein, which is essential for muscle maintenance and repair, particularly important for individuals on dialysis.
- **Low in Sodium:** This recipe is naturally low in sodium, which is beneficial for managing fluid balance and blood pressure.

- **Antioxidant-Rich:** Fresh berries are rich in antioxidants, vitamins, and fiber, contributing to overall health and supporting immune function.
- **Digestive Health:** Greek yogurt contains probiotics that promote gut health and support a balanced digestive system. The addition of chia seeds provides extra fiber, aiding in digestion and maintaining regular bowel movements.
- **Versatile and Customizable:** This recipe can be easily customized with various fruits, seeds, or nuts to suit your taste preferences and dietary needs.

5. Banana Smoothie with Flaxseed

Preparation Time

- **5 minutes**

Cooking Time

- **None**

Serving Unit

- **2 servings**

Ingredients

- **1 large ripe banana**
- **1 cup unsweetened almond milk** (or any other low-potassium, low-phosphorus milk alternative)
- **1 tablespoon ground flaxseeds**
- **1/2 teaspoon vanilla extract** (optional, for added flavor)
- **1/2 teaspoon cinnamon** (optional, for extra flavor)
- **Ice cubes** (optional, for a colder smoothie)

Procedures of Preparation

1. **Prepare the Banana:**
   - Peel the banana and cut it into chunks.
2. **Combine Ingredients:**
   - In a blender, add the banana chunks, unsweetened almond milk, and ground flaxseeds. If using, add the vanilla extract and cinnamon for added flavor.
3. **Blend Smoothie:**
   - Blend on high speed until smooth and creamy. If you prefer a colder smoothie, add a few ice cubes to the blender and blend again until well combined and chilled.
4. **Serve:**
   - Pour the smoothie into two glasses. Serve immediately

for optimal texture and taste.

Nutritional Values (Per Serving)

- **Calories:** 150
- **Protein:** 4g
- **Carbohydrates:** 30g
- **Fat:** 5g
- **Sodium:** 90mg
- **Potassium:** 300mg
- **Phosphorus:** 80mg

Note: Nutritional values are approximate and can vary based on specific ingredient brands and quantities used.

Cooking Tips

- **Use Ripe Bananas:** Choose ripe bananas for the best natural sweetness and smoothest texture in your smoothie.
- **Ground Flaxseeds:** Use ground flaxseeds rather than whole flaxseeds to ensure that your body can absorb their nutrients effectively.
- **Adjust Sweetness:** If you prefer a sweeter smoothie, you can add a small amount of honey or maple syrup, but be mindful of additional sugars.
- **Add Ice for Texture:** If you like a colder and thicker smoothie, add ice cubes before blending. You can also use frozen banana slices to achieve a similar effect.
- **Blend Thoroughly:** Ensure you blend the smoothie thoroughly to achieve a smooth, even consistency without lumps.

Health Benefits

- **Rich in Fiber:** Flaxseeds are an excellent source of dietary fiber, which aids in digestion, supports heart health, and helps maintain regular bowel movements.
- **Heart-Healthy:** Flaxseeds contain omega-3 fatty acids, which are beneficial for heart health and can help reduce inflammation.
- **Low in Sodium:** This smoothie is naturally low in sodium, making it suitable for those managing blood pressure and fluid balance.
- **Potassium Control:** While bananas do contain potassium, using one banana in the recipe helps keep the potassium levels within a manageable range for those on a kidney-friendly diet.
- **Digestive Health:** The combination of banana and flaxseeds promotes digestive health. Flaxseeds are particularly effective in supporting healthy bowel function and reducing constipation.
- **Nutrient-Dense:** This smoothie provides essential vitamins and minerals, including vitamin C

from the banana and a range of nutrients from the flaxseeds, contributing to overall well-being.

6. Cottage Cheese with Pineapple

Preparation Time

- **5 minutes**

Cooking Time

- **None**

Serving Unit

- **2 servings**

Ingredients

- **1 cup low-fat cottage cheese**
- **1/2 cup fresh pineapple chunks** (or canned pineapple in its own juice, drained)
- **1 tablespoon honey** (optional, for extra sweetness)
- **¼ of teaspoon vanilla extract (optional for extra flavor)**
-
- **1 tablespoon chopped nuts** (such as almonds or walnuts, optional for added crunch)

Procedures of Preparation

1. **Prepare the Pineapple:**
   - If using fresh pineapple, peel, core, and chop into bite-sized pieces. If using canned pineapple, drain it well to remove excess juice.
2. **Combine Ingredients:**
   - In a medium bowl, add 1 cup of low-fat cottage cheese.
3. **Mix Pineapple and Optional Ingredients:**
   - Gently fold the pineapple chunks into the cottage cheese.
   - If desired, stir in the honey and vanilla extract for added sweetness and flavor.
4. **Add Optional Toppings:**

- Sprinkle the chopped nuts on top if using, for additional texture and a touch of healthy fats.

5. **Serve:**
    - Divide the mixture between two bowls. Refrigerate until ready to eat, or serve immediately.

Nutritional Values (Per Serving)

- **Calories:** 170
- **Protein:** 15g
- **Carbohydrates:** 20g
- **Fat:** 3g
- **Sodium:** 300mg
- **Potassium:** 250mg
- **Phosphorus:** 180mg

Note: Nutritional values are approximate and can vary based on specific ingredient brands and quantities used.

Cooking Tips

- **Use Low-Fat Cottage Cheese:** Opt for low-fat or fat-free cottage cheese to keep the recipe lower in fat while still providing a good source of protein.
- **Adjust Sweetness:** If the pineapple is sweet enough on its own, you may not need the honey. Adjust according to your taste preference.
- **Choose Fresh Pineapple:** Fresh pineapple offers a vibrant flavor and texture, but canned pineapple can be a convenient alternative. Make sure to choose pineapple packed in its own juice rather than syrup to keep it lower in added sugars.
- **Mix Gently:** Fold the pineapple into the cottage cheese gently to avoid breaking down the fruit and to maintain a pleasant texture.
- **Chill Before Serving:** For a refreshing treat, chill the cottage cheese and pineapple mixture in the refrigerator for about 30 minutes before serving.

Health Benefits

- **High in Protein:** Cottage cheese is an excellent source of protein, which is crucial for muscle repair and overall body function. It helps keep you feeling full and supports muscle maintenance, particularly important for individuals on dialysis.
- **Low in Fat:** Using low-fat cottage cheese reduces the overall fat content of the dish while still providing essential nutrients.
- **Rich in Vitamins:** Pineapple is rich in vitamin C, an antioxidant that supports immune function and helps with collagen production for healthy skin and tissues.

- **Digestive Health:** Pineapple contains bromelain, an enzyme that aids digestion and may help reduce inflammation in the digestive tract.
- **Balanced Nutrients:** The combination of cottage cheese and pineapple provides a balanced mix of protein, carbohydrates, and vitamins while being relatively low in sodium, potassium, and phosphorus compared to many other dairy and fruit options.

7. Chia Seed Pudding with Apple

Preparation Time

- **5 minutes**

Cooking Time

- **None**

Chilling Time

- **4 hours (or overnight)**

Serving Unit

- **2 servings**

Ingredients

- **1/4 cup chia seeds**
- **1 cup unsweetened almond milk** (or any other low-potassium, low-phosphorus milk alternative)
- **1 tablespoon of maple syrup (or honey, optional for sweetness)**
- **1/2 teaspoon vanilla extract** (optional, for added flavor)
- **1 medium apple** (such as Fuji or Gala), peeled, cored, and diced
- **1/2 teaspoon ground cinnamon (optional, to add taste)**
- **1 tablespoon chopped walnuts** (optional, for added crunch)

Procedures of Preparation

1. **Prepare Chia Seed Mixture:**
   - In a medium bowl or jar, combine 1/4 cup chia seeds with 1 cup unsweetened almond milk.
   - Stir in the maple syrup and vanilla extract if using. Mix well to achieve an evenly distribution of the chia seeds
2. **Chill:**
   - Cover the bowl or jar and refrigerate for at least 4 hours, or overnight. This allows the chia seeds to absorb the liquid and

expand, forming a pudding-like consistency.

3. **Prepare the Apple:**
   - While the chia pudding is chilling, peel, core, and dice the apple into small pieces. If you prefer, you can lightly sauté the apple pieces in a non-stick pan with a pinch of cinnamon for added flavor, though this step is optional.
4. **Assemble:**
   - Once the chia pudding has set, stir it well to ensure an even consistency. Spoon the pudding into serving bowls.
   - Top each serving with the diced apple. Sprinkle with ground cinnamon and chopped walnuts if desired.
5. **Serve:**
   - Serve immediately, or chill for an additional 30 minutes for a colder treat.

Nutritional Values (Per Serving)

- **Calories:** 180
- **Protein:** 5g
- **Carbohydrates:** 24g
- **Fat:** 8g
- **Sodium:** 55mg
- **Potassium:** 300mg
- **Phosphorus:** 120mg

Note: Nutritional values are approximate and can vary based on specific ingredient brands and quantities used.

Cooking Tips

- **Ensure Proper Mixing:** When preparing the chia seed mixture, ensure that the chia seeds are well-distributed and not clumping together. Stirring the mixture a few times during the first hour of chilling can help prevent clumps.
- **Customize Sweetness:** Adjust the amount of maple syrup or honey according to your taste preferences. For a lower sugar option, you can use a small amount or omit the sweetener.
- **Use Fresh Apples:** Fresh apples add a crisp texture and natural sweetness to the pudding. If you prefer a softer texture, consider sautéing the apples briefly before adding them to the pudding.
- **Top Before Serving:** For the best texture and flavor, add the apple topping just before serving to keep the apples fresh and crunchy.

Health Benefits

- **Rich in Omega-3s:** Chia seeds are an excellent source of omega-3 fatty acids, which are beneficial for heart health and reducing inflammation.

- **High in Fiber:** Chia seeds are packed with dietary fiber, which supports digestive health and helps maintain regular bowel movements.
- **Low in Sodium and Phosphorus:** This recipe is naturally low in sodium and phosphorus, making it suitable for individuals with kidney concerns.
- **Antioxidant-Rich:** Apples are rich in antioxidants, including vitamin C, which supports immune health and helps protect cells from damage.
- **Blood Sugar Regulation:** The combination of chia seeds and apples can help stabilize blood sugar levels, thanks to the fiber content in both ingredients.

2

Lunches

8. Grilled Chicken Salad with Lemon Vinaigrette

Preparation Time

- **15 minutes**

Cooking Time

- **10 minutes**

Serving Unit

- **2 servings**

Ingredients

For the Salad:

- **2 boneless, skinless chicken breasts**
- **4 cups mixed salad greens (including spinach, arugula, and romaine)**
- **1 cup cherry tomatoes**, halved
- **1/2 cucumber**, sliced
- **1/4 red onion**, thinly sliced
- **1/4 cup shredded carrots**
- **1/4 cup of sliced bell peppers, red or yellow**

For the Lemon Vinaigrette:

- **2 tablespoons olive oil**
- **1 tablespoon freshly squeezed lemon juice**
- **1 teaspoon Dijon mustard**
- **1 clove garlic**, minced
- **1/2 teaspoon honey** (optional, for added sweetness)
- **Salt and pepper** to taste (use sparingly to keep sodium low)

Procedures of Preparation

1. **Prepare the Chicken:**
    - Preheat the grill or grill pan on a medium to high heat.
    - Season the chicken breasts with a small amount of salt and pepper. Optionally, you can add herbs like rosemary or thyme for extra flavor.
    - Grill the chicken for about 5 minutes on each side or

until fully cooked and the internal temperature reaches 165°F (75°C). The chicken should be moist and have nice grill masks.

2. **Prepare the Lemon Vinaigrette:**
   - In a small bowl, whisk together the olive oil, lemon juice, Dijon mustard, minced garlic, and honey if using. Season with a bit of pepper and a pinch of salt to taste.
3. **Assemble the Salad:**
   - Prepare the salad ingredients while the chicken is grilling. In a large bowl, combine the mixed greens, cherry tomatoes, cucumber slices, red onion, shredded carrots, and bell peppers.
   - Allow the cooked chicken to rest for a few minutes before slicing it into strips.
   - Add the sliced chicken to the salad bowl.
4. **Dress the Salad:**
   - Sprinkle the lemon vinaigrette on the salad just before serving. Toss gently to ensure that the dressing is evenly distributed.
5. **Serve:**
   - Divide the salad into two bowls or plates and serve immediately.

Nutritional Values (Per Serving)

- **Calories:** 300
- **Protein:** 30g
- **Carbohydrates:** 15g
- **Fat:** 15g
- **Sodium:** 300mg
- **Potassium:** 600mg
- **Phosphorus:** 200mg

Note: Nutritional values are approximate and can vary based on specific ingredient brands and quantities used.

Cooking Tips

- **Grilling Chicken:** To ensure even cooking, flatten the chicken breasts to an even thickness before grilling. This helps them cook more uniformly.
- **Marinate for Flavor:** For extra flavor, marinate the chicken in a mixture of olive oil, lemon juice, and herbs for 30 minutes before grilling.
- **Use Fresh Ingredients:** Fresh, crisp vegetables will enhance the salad's flavor and texture. Opt for seasonal produce when possible.
- **Adjust Dressing:** If you prefer a lighter dressing, reduce the amount of olive oil or increase the lemon juice. You can also use a sugar substitute instead of honey if you're watching your sugar intake.
- **Rest the Chicken:** Allow the grilled chicken to rest for a few

minutes before slicing. This helps retain the juices and keeps the chicken moist.

Health Benefits

- **Lean Protein Source:** Grilled chicken is a lean source of protein that supports muscle maintenance and overall body function while being relatively low in fat and calories.
- **Low Sodium and Phosphorus:** This salad is naturally low in sodium and phosphorus, making it suitable for those managing kidney health.
- **Rich in Vitamins and Minerals:** The fresh vegetables in the salad provide a range of vitamins and minerals, including vitamins A and C, potassium, and antioxidants.
- **Healthy Fats:** Olive oil is a source of monounsaturated fats, which are beneficial for heart health and can help reduce inflammation.
- **Digestive Health:** The fiber from the vegetables and the chicken helps promote healthy digestion and may aid in maintaining a healthy weight.

9. Turkey and Avocado Wraps

Preparation Time

- **10 minutes**

Cooking Time

- **None**

Serving Unit

- **2 servings**

Ingredients

- **4 whole wheat or low-sodium tortillas** (preferably soft and flexible)
- **8 oz sliced turkey breast** (preferably low-sodium and nitrate-free)
- **1 ripe avocado,** sliced
- **1 cup baby spinach** (or other leafy greens such as kale or arugula)
- **1/2 cup shredded carrots**
- **1/2 red bell pepper**, thinly sliced
- **1/4 cup thinly sliced red onion**
- **2 tablespoons hummus** (optional, for added flavor and creaminess)
- **1 tablespoon lemon juice (optional, to keep avocado from browning)**
- **Salt and pepper** to taste (use sparingly to keep sodium low)
- **Fresh herbs** (optional, such as cilantro or basil for extra flavor)

Procedures of Preparation

1. **Prepare Ingredients:**
    - Wash and slice the avocado, then drizzle with lemon juice if desired to prevent browning.
    - Cut the onion and red bell pepper thinly. Shred the carrots if not pre-shredded.
2. **Prepare Tortillas:**

- Warm the tortillas slightly in a dry skillet over medium heat or in the microwave for about 20 seconds. This makes them softer and simpler to roll.

3. **Assemble the Wraps:**
   - Lay out the tortillas on a clean surface. If using, spread 1/2 tablespoon of hummus evenly over each tortilla.
   - Arrange a few slices of turkey breast in the center of each tortilla.
   - Layer the avocado slices, baby spinach, shredded carrots, red bell pepper, and red onion on top of the turkey.
4. **Season:**
   - Season with a bit of pepper and a pinch of salt if desired. Add fresh herbs if using.
5. **Wrap and Slice:**
   - Fold in the sides of each tortilla and roll tightly from one end to the other. Slice each wrap in half diagonally for easier handling and presentation.
6. **Serve:**
   - Serve immediately, or wrap in plastic wrap or foil and refrigerate for up to 2 hours if preparing in advance.

Nutritional Values (Per Serving)

- **Calories:** 300
- **Protein:** 25g
- **Carbohydrates:** 30g
- **Fat:** 12g
- **Sodium:** 400mg
- **Potassium:** 600mg
- **Phosphorus:** 250mg

Note: Nutritional values are approximate and can vary based on specific ingredient brands and quantities used.

Cooking Tips

- **Use Fresh Ingredients:** Use fresh, high-quality ingredients to achieve the finest taste and texture. Fresh vegetables and ripe avocados enhance the taste and nutritional value of the wraps.
- **Warm Tortillas:** Warming the tortillas before assembling makes them more flexible and easier to roll without tearing.
- **Adjust Fillings:** Customize the wraps by adding other vegetables or spreads that suit your taste and dietary needs. For example, try adding cucumber slices or using a different type of leafy green.
- **Prevent Avocado Browning:** To keep the avocado fresh and green, use lemon juice and store the wraps in an airtight container if making them ahead of time.

Health Benefits

- **Lean Protein Source:** Turkey is a lean source of protein that supports muscle maintenance and overall health while being low in fat and calories.
- **Healthy Fats:** Avocado provides heart-healthy monounsaturated fats, which can help reduce inflammation and support cardiovascular health.
- **Nutrient-Rich Vegetables:** The addition of vegetables such as spinach, carrots, bell peppers, and onions adds vitamins, minerals, and fiber to the wraps, supporting digestive health and overall well-being.
- **Low Sodium:** By using low-sodium tortillas and turkey, this recipe helps maintain low sodium levels, which is beneficial for blood pressure and kidney health.
- **Potassium and Phosphorus Balance:** The ingredients are balanced to offer a moderate amount of potassium and phosphorus, making the wraps suitable for those managing these levels.

10. Roasted Vegetable Soup

Preparation Time

- **15 minutes**

Cooking Time

- **45 minutes**

Serving Unit

- **4 servings**

Ingredients

- **2 big carrots, peeled and cut into bits**
- **1 medium zucchini**, sliced
- **1 red bell pepper**, deseeded and chopped
- **1 yellow bell pepper**, deseeded and chopped
- **1 medium onion**, quartered
- **2 cloves garlic**, peeled and left whole
- **2 tablespoons olive oil**
- **1 teaspoon dried thyme**
- **1 teaspoon dried basil**
- **Salt and pepper** to taste (use sparingly to keep sodium low)
- **4 cups low-sodium vegetable broth**
- **1 cup water**
- **1 bay leaf**
- **Fresh parsley** (optional, for garnish)

Procedures of Preparation

1. **Preheat the Oven:**
    - Preheat your oven to 400°F (200°C).
2. **Prepare the Vegetables:**
    - Place the carrots, zucchini, red and yellow bell peppers, onion, and garlic on a large baking sheet. Drizzle with olive oil and sprinkle with dried thyme, dried basil, salt, and pepper. Toss the veggies to ensure they are equally

covered with oil and spices.

3. **Roast the Vegetables:**
    - Roast the vegetables in the preheated oven for 25-30 minutes, or until they are tender and slightly caramelized, stirring halfway through the cooking time for even roasting.
4. **Simmer the Soup:**
    - In a large pot, combine the roasted vegetables, low-sodium vegetable broth, water, and bay leaf. Bring the mixture to a boil over medium-high heat, then reduce the heat to low and let it simmer for 15 minutes, allowing the flavors to meld together.
5. **Blend the Soup:**
    - Remove the bay leaf from the pot. Use an immersion blender to slowly blend the soup until smooth. If you prefer a chunkier texture, you can blend only part of the soup, leaving some of the vegetables whole.
    - Alternatively, transfer the soup in batches to a countertop blender, blending until smooth, and then return it to the pot.
6. **Adjust Seasoning:**
    - Taste the soup and adjust the seasoning as needed, adding more salt or pepper if desired. If the soup is too thick, you can add a little more water or broth to reach your desired consistency.
7. **Serve:**
    - Ladle the soup into bowls and garnish with fresh parsley if using. Serve hot with a slice of crusty bread or a simple side salad.

Nutritional Values (Per Serving)

- **Calories:** 120
- **Protein:** 3g
- **Carbohydrates:** 20g
- **Fat:** 5g
- **Sodium:** 200mg
- **Potassium:** 500mg
- **Phosphorus:** 90mg

Note: Nutritional values are approximate and can vary based on specific ingredient brands and quantities used.

Cooking Tips

- **Roast for Flavor:** Roasting the vegetables intensifies their natural flavors, adding a rich, sweet undertone to the soup. Make sure to spread the vegetables out in a single layer on the baking sheet for even roasting.
- **Customize the Vegetables:** Feel free to customize the

vegetables in the soup based on what you have on hand. Root vegetables like sweet potatoes or parsnips can be added for a heartier texture.

- **Blending Safety:** When blending hot liquids, be cautious to avoid splatters. If using a countertop blender, blend in small batches and leave the lid slightly open to allow steam to escape.
- **Add Fresh Herbs:** Fresh herbs like thyme, rosemary, or parsley can be added during the final simmer for added freshness and complexity.

Health Benefits

- **Rich in Antioxidants:** The variety of colorful vegetables used in this soup provides a wealth of antioxidants, which help protect your cells from damage caused by free radicals.
- **Low in Sodium:** This recipe uses low-sodium vegetable broth and minimal added salt, making it suitable for those managing sodium intake, especially for kidney health.
- **High in Fiber:** The vegetables in this soup are naturally high in dietary fiber, which aids in digestion and helps maintain healthy blood sugar levels.
- **Hydrating:** The high water content in the soup contributes to hydration, which is crucial for kidney function and overall health.
- **Heart-Healthy Fats:** Olive oil adds a source of healthy monounsaturated fats, which are beneficial for cardiovascular health and can help reduce inflammation.

11. Quinoa and Black Bean Salad

Preparation Time

- **15 minutes**

Cooking Time

- **15 minutes** (for quinoa)

Serving Unit

- **4 servings**

Ingredients

- **1 cup quinoa**, rinsed
- **2 cups water**
- **1 can (15 oz) black beans**, drained and rinsed (low-sodium or no-salt-added)
- **1 cup cherry tomatoes**, halved
- **1 small red bell pepper**, diced
- **1/2 small red onion**, finely chopped
- **1/2 cup fresh cilantro**, chopped
- **1/4 cup lime juice** (about 2 limes)
- **2 tablespoons olive oil**
- **1 teaspoon ground cumin**
- **1/2 teaspoon chili powder**
- **Salt and pepper** to taste (use sparingly to keep sodium low)
- **Optional toppings:** diced avocado, crumbled feta cheese (if dairy is permitted)

Procedures of Preparation

1. **Cook the Quinoa:**
   - In a medium saucepan, mix the rinsed quinoa and water. Bring to a boil over a medium to high heat.
   - Once boiling, reduce the heat to low, cover the saucepan, and simmer for about 15 minutes, or until the quinoa has absorbed all the water and is tender. Remove from fire and allow to settle for 5 minutes, covered, before

fluffing with a fork. Allow the quinoa to cool slightly.

2. **Prepare the Vegetables:**
    - While the quinoa is cooking, prepare the vegetables. Finely chop the red onion and cilantro, halve the cherry tomatoes and dice the red bell pepper.
3. **Mix the Salad:**
    - In a large bowl, combine the cooked quinoa, black beans, cherry tomatoes, red bell pepper, red onion, and cilantro. Toss gently to mix.
4. **Make the Dressing:**
    - In a small bowl, combine the lime juice, olive oil, powdered cumin, chili powder, salt, and pepper. Adjust seasoning to taste, keeping in mind the sodium content.
5. **Dress the Salad:**
    - Pour the dressing over the quinoa-vegetable combination. Toss until everything is evenly coated.
6. **Serve:**
    - Refrigerate for an hour to allow the flavors to combine or serve immediately. Optionally, top with diced avocado or crumbled feta cheese before serving.

Nutritional Values (Per Serving)

- **Calories:** 250
- **Protein:** 8g
- **Carbohydrates:** 35g
- **Fat:** 8g
- **Sodium:** 150mg
- **Potassium:** 600mg
- **Phosphorus:** 200mg

Note: Nutritional values are approximate and can vary based on specific ingredient brands and quantities used.

Cooking Tips

- **Rinse the Quinoa:** Always rinse quinoa under cold water before cooking to remove the natural coating called saponin, which can have a bitter taste.
- **Cool the Quinoa:** Allow the quinoa to cool slightly before adding it to the salad to prevent wilting the vegetables and to help the salad maintain a good texture.
- **Customize the Vegetables:** Feel free to add or substitute other kidney-friendly vegetables, such as cucumbers or radishes, based on your preferences and what's available.
- **Make Ahead:** This salad can be made ahead of time and stored in the refrigerator for up to 2 days. The flavors will deepen as it sits, making it a great option for meal prep.

- **Add Toppings:** For extra richness, consider adding toppings like diced avocado or a sprinkle of feta cheese if your diet allows. However, remember to account for any additional sodium or phosphorus these toppings might add.

Health Benefits

- **Complete Protein:** Quinoa is one of the few plant-based foods that provide all nine essential amino acids, making it an excellent source of complete protein, especially important for individuals on dialysis who need to manage protein intake.
- **High in Fiber:** Black beans and quinoa are both high in dietary fiber, which supports digestive health and helps maintain stable blood sugar levels.
- **Rich in Antioxidants:** The fresh vegetables and herbs in this salad provide a variety of antioxidants, which protect your cells from damage and support overall health.
- **Low in Sodium:** This recipe uses low-sodium ingredients and minimal added salt, making it suitable for those managing their sodium intake to protect kidney function.
- **Heart-Healthy Fats:** Olive oil adds a source of monounsaturated fats, which are beneficial for heart health and can help reduce inflammation.

12. Baked Cod with Steamed Broccoli

Preparation Time

- **10 minutes**

Cooking Time

- **20 minutes**

Serving Unit

- **2 servings**

Ingredients

- **2 cod fillets** (about 6 oz each)
- **1 tablespoon olive oil**
- **1 tablespoon lemon juice** (about 1/2 a lemon)
- **1 clove garlic**, minced
- **1 teaspoon dried thyme**
- **1 teaspoon dried parsley**
- **Salt and pepper** to taste (use sparingly to keep sodium low)
- **1 medium head broccoli chopped into florets**
- **1 tablespoon unsalted butter** (optional, for broccoli)

Procedures of Preparation

1. **Preheat the Oven:**
   - Preheat your oven to 400°F (200°C). Line a baking sheet with parchment paper or gently coat it with olive oil.
2. **Prepare the Cod:**
   - To eliminate extra moisture, pat dry the cod fillets using paper towels. Put the fillets on the prepared baking sheet.
3. **Season the Cod:**
   - In a small bowl, mix together the olive oil, lemon juice, minced garlic, dried thyme, dried parsley, salt, and pepper. Brush this mixture evenly over the cod fillets, making sure to coat both sides.
4. **Bake the Cod:**

  - Place the baking sheet in the preheated oven and bake for 12-15 minutes, or until the cod is opaque and flakes easily with a fork. The actual cooking time varies according to the thickness of the fillets.
5. **Steam the Broccoli:**
  - While the cod is baking, prepare the broccoli. Boil a pot of water and set a steamer basket over it.. Add the broccoli florets to the steamer basket, cover, and steam for 5-7 minutes, or until the broccoli is tender but still bright green.
6. **Serve:**
  - Divide the baked cod and steamed broccoli between two plates. If desired, drizzle the broccoli with a small amount of melted unsalted butter for added flavor.

Nutritional Values (Per Serving)

- **Calories:** 250
- **Protein:** 28g
- **Carbohydrates:** 7g
- **Fat:** 11g
- **Sodium:** 150mg
- **Potassium:** 900mg
- **Phosphorus:** 300mg

Note: Nutritional values are approximate and can vary based on specific ingredient brands and quantities used.

Cooking Tips

- **Check for Doneness:** Cod is a delicate fish, so it's important not to overcook it. The fish is done when it flakes easily with a fork and becomes opaque.
- **Add Fresh Herbs:** For a burst of fresh flavor, consider adding fresh herbs like dill or parsley to the cod after baking. These herbs not only enhance the taste but also add visual appeal.
- **Customize the Vegetables:** While broccoli is a great pairing, you can easily substitute or add other kidney-friendly vegetables like cauliflower or asparagus.
- **Avoid Overcooking the Broccoli:** To maintain the vibrant color and nutrients of the broccoli, steam it just until tender. Overcooking might result in a mushy texture and loss of nutrients.
- **Butter Substitute:** If you want to avoid butter, you can drizzle the steamed broccoli with a little olive oil or lemon juice instead.

Health Benefits

- **High in Lean Protein:** Cod is a lean source of high-quality protein, which is essential for maintaining muscle mass and supporting overall health, especially for those on dialysis.

- **Low in Sodium:** This recipe uses minimal added salt, making it suitable for individuals who need to manage their sodium intake to support kidney health.
- **Rich in Omega-3 Fatty Acids:** Cod is a good source of omega-3 fatty acids, which are known for their anti-inflammatory properties and support cardiovascular health.
- **Packed with Antioxidants:** Broccoli is rich in antioxidants, including vitamin C and sulforaphane, which help protect the body from oxidative stress and support immune function.
- **Supports Bone Health:** Both cod and broccoli are good sources of phosphorus and potassium, which are important for maintaining strong bones and proper muscle function. However, these nutrients are present in moderate amounts, making this dish balanced for kidney health.
- **Low in Calories:** This meal is low in calories but high in nutrients, making it an excellent choice for those looking to maintain a healthy weight while ensuring they get essential nutrients.

13. Sweet Potato and Lentil Stew

Preparation Time

- **15 minutes**

Cooking Time

- **45 minutes**

Serving Unit

- **4 servings**

Ingredients

- **1 tablespoon olive oil**
- **1 medium onion**, chopped
- **2 cloves garlic**, minced
- **1 teaspoon ground cumin**
- **1 teaspoon ground coriander**
- **1/2 teaspoon smoked paprika**
- **1/4 teaspoon turmeric**
- **1 cup of either dried green or brown lentils, rinsed and drained**
- **2 medium sweet potatoes**, peeled and diced (about 3 cups)
- **1 can (14.5 oz) diced tomatoes**, no-salt-added
- **4 cups low-sodium vegetable broth**
- **1 bay leaf**
- **1 teaspoon fresh thyme** or **1/2 teaspoon dried thyme**
- **Salt and pepper** to taste (use sparingly to keep sodium low)
- **2 cups fresh spinach** (optional, for added greens)
- **Fresh cilantro** for garnish (optional)

Procedures of Preparation

1. **Sauté the Aromatics:**
   - In a big pot or Dutch oven warm the olive oil over medium heat. Add the chopped onion and sauté for about 5 minutes, or until the onion is soft and translucent.

  - Add the minced garlic, ground cumin, ground coriander, smoked paprika, and turmeric to the pot. Stir and cook for another 1-2 minutes until the spices are fragrant.
2. **Add Lentils and Sweet Potatoes:**
   - Stir in the lentils, diced sweet potatoes, and diced tomatoes. Mix well to coat the lentils and sweet potatoes with the spice mixture.
3. **Simmer the Stew:**
   - Pour in the low-sodium vegetable broth and add the bay leaf and thyme. Boil the mixture over high heat.
   - Once boiling, reduce the heat to low, cover the pot, and simmer for about 30-35 minutes, or until the lentils are tender and the sweet potatoes are soft.
4. **Season the Stew:**
   - Taste the stew and season with salt and pepper as required. If using fresh spinach, stir it in during the last 5 minutes of cooking until it wilts.
5. **Serve:**
   - Remove the bay leaf before serving. Ladle the stew into bowls and garnish with fresh cilantro if desired. Serve hot with fresh bread or a small salad.

Nutritional Values (Per Serving)

- **Calories:** 300
- **Protein:** 12g
- **Carbohydrates:** 50g
- **Fat:** 5g
- **Sodium:** 150mg
- **Potassium:** 900mg
- **Phosphorus:** 200mg
- **Fiber:** 12g

Note: Nutritional values are approximate and can vary based on specific ingredient brands and quantities used.

Cooking Tips

- **Choose the Right Lentils:** Green or brown lentils work best for this recipe as they hold their shape during cooking. Red lentils tend to break down and create a more mushy texture, which can also be pleasant but will alter the consistency of the stew.
- **Adjust the Thickness:** If you prefer a thicker stew, reduce the amount of vegetable broth slightly or simmer the stew uncovered for the last 10 minutes of cooking. For a thinner consistency, add a bit more broth or water as needed.

- **Boost the Vegetables:** Feel free to add other kidney-friendly vegetables like carrots, zucchini, or bell peppers to increase the nutrient content and add more variety to the stew.
- **Store for Later:** This stew keeps well in the refrigerator for up to 4 days and can be frozen for up to 3 months. Reheat gently on the stovetop, adding a splash of water or broth if needed to restore the desired consistency.
- **Enhance the Flavor:** A squeeze of fresh lemon juice before serving can brighten the flavors and add a nice contrast to the earthy stew.

Health Benefits

- **Rich in Plant-Based Protein:** Lentils are an excellent source of plant-based protein, providing essential amino acids that help maintain muscle mass and support overall health, especially for those on a plant-forward diet.
- **High in Fiber:** Both lentils and sweet potatoes are rich in dietary fiber, which aids in digestion, helps regulate blood sugar levels, and promotes a feeling of fullness, making this stew particularly satisfying.
- **Low in Sodium:** The recipe uses low-sodium vegetable broth and minimal added salt, making it suitable for individuals managing their sodium intake to protect kidney function.
- **Packed with Vitamins and Minerals:** Sweet potatoes are rich in vitamins A and C, which support immune function and skin health. Lentils provide important minerals like iron, phosphorus, and potassium, which are essential for energy production, bone health, and muscle function.
- **Anti-Inflammatory Properties:** The spices used, such as turmeric and cumin, have anti-inflammatory properties that can help reduce inflammation in the body, supporting overall health and well-being.
- **Heart-Healthy Fats:** Olive oil adds a source of monounsaturated fats, which are beneficial for heart health and can help reduce inflammation.

14. Spinach and Mushroom Frittata

Preparation Time

- **10 minutes**

Cooking Time

- **20 minutes**

Serving Unit

- **4 servings**

Ingredients

- **8 large eggs**
- **1/4 cup low-fat milk** (optional, for a creamier texture)
- **1 tablespoon olive oil**
- **1 small onion**, finely chopped
- **2 cloves garlic**, minced
- **1 cup mushrooms**, sliced (white or cremini mushrooms work well)
- **2 cups fresh spinach**, roughly chopped
- **1/4 cup grated Parmesan cheese** (optional, for added flavor and protein)
- **Salt and pepper** to taste (use sparingly to keep sodium low)
- **Fresh herbs such as chives or parsley (optional, for garnish)**

Procedures of Preparation

1. **Preheat the Oven:**
    - Preheat your oven to 350°F (175°C). If you have an oven-safe skillet, you can use it for the entire process. Otherwise, prepare a baking dish by lightly greasing it with olive oil.
2. **Prepare the Egg Mixture:**
    - In a large bowl, whisk together the eggs and low-fat milk (if using). For seasoning, add a dash of both pepper and salt. Set aside.

3. **Sauté the Vegetables:**
   - In a large oven-safe skillet, heat the olive oil on medium heat. Add the chopped onion and sauté for about 3-4 minutes, or until it becomes soft and translucent.
   - To the pan, add the sliced mushrooms and minced garlic. Cook for another 5 minutes, stirring occasionally, until the mushrooms are tender and have released their moisture.
   - Add the chopped spinach to the skillet and cook for 2-3 minutes, until the spinach has wilted.
4. **Combine and Cook:**
   - Spread the sautéed vegetables evenly in the skillet. Pour the egg mixture over the vegetables, ensuring everything is evenly distributed. If using Parmesan cheese, sprinkle it on top.
   - Cook on the stovetop over medium-low heat for 3-4 minutes, or until the edges start to set.
5. **Bake the Frittata:**
   - Transfer the skillet to the preheated oven and bake for 10-12 minutes, or until the frittata is fully set in the center and lightly golden on top. If using a baking dish, pour the mixture into the prepared dish and bake for the same amount of time.
   - Once done, take it out of the oven and allow it to cool down before slicing.
6. **Serve:**
   - Cut the frittata into wedges and serve warm, garnished with fresh herbs if desired. This frittata pairs well with a simple side salad or whole-grain toast.

Nutritional Values (Per Serving)

- **Calories:** 180
- **Protein:** 12g
- **Carbohydrates:** 4g
- **Fat:** 12g
- **Sodium:** 180mg
- **Potassium:** 300mg
- **Phosphorus:** 180mg

Note: Nutritional values are approximate and can vary based on specific ingredient brands and quantities used.

Cooking Tips

- **Use an Oven-Safe Skillet:** If you don't have an oven-safe skillet, you can transfer the sautéed vegetables to a baking dish before adding the egg mixture. Just make sure to grease the baking dish lightly to prevent sticking.

- **Add More Vegetables:** Feel free to add other kidney-friendly vegetables to the frittata, such as bell peppers, zucchini, or tomatoes, to increase the nutrient content and add variety.
- **Cheese Substitute:** If you prefer to avoid dairy, you can skip the Parmesan cheese or use a dairy-free alternative. Nutritional yeast is a great option that provides a cheesy flavor without the added sodium.
- **Make It Ahead:** This frittata can be made ahead of time and stored in the refrigerator for up to 3 days. For a fast and easy meal, you may microwave individual pieces again or eat them cold.
- **Serving Suggestions:** Serve the frittata with a side of fresh fruit, whole-grain toast, or a small salad for a balanced meal. It also pairs well with a light yogurt dip or salsa.

Health Benefits

- **High in Protein:** Eggs are an excellent source of high-quality protein, which is essential for maintaining muscle mass and overall health. This makes the frittata a great option for those on dialysis who need to ensure adequate protein intake.
- **Low in Sodium:** This recipe uses minimal added salt, making it suitable for individuals who need to manage their sodium intake. The natural flavors of the vegetables and herbs provide plenty of taste without the need for excessive salt.
- **Rich in Vitamins and Minerals:** Spinach is packed with vitamins A, C, and K, as well as folate and iron, which support immune function, bone health, and red blood cell production. Mushrooms add a dose of B vitamins and antioxidants.
- **Supports Heart Health:** The use of olive oil in this recipe provides heart-healthy monounsaturated fats, which can help reduce inflammation and support cardiovascular health.
- **Aids in Weight Management:** The combination of protein and fiber in this frittata helps promote satiety, making it a satisfying meal that can aid in weight management by keeping you full for longer periods.
- **Low in Carbohydrates:** This frittata is low in carbohydrates, making it a suitable option for those who need to manage their blood sugar levels or follow a low-carb diet.

3

Dinners

15. Herb-Crusted Salmon with Asparagus

Preparation Time

- **10 minutes**

Cooking Time

- **20 minutes**

Serving Unit

- **4 servings**

Ingredients

- **4 salmon fillets** (about 4-6 oz each)
- **1 tablespoon olive oil**
- **1 tablespoon Dijon mustard**
- **1/2 cup panko breadcrumbs**
- **2 tablespoons fresh parsley**, finely chopped
- **2 tablespoons fresh dill**, finely chopped
- **2 cloves garlic**, minced
- **Zest of 1 lemon**
- **Salt and pepper** to taste (use sparingly to keep sodium low)
- **1 bunch asparagus**, trimmed
- **1 tablespoon lemon juice**
- **1/2 teaspoon lemon zest** for garnish (optional)

Procedures of Preparation

1. **Preheat the Oven:**
   - Preheat your oven to 400°F (200°C). Line a baking sheet with parchment paper or gently coat it with olive oil.
2. **Prepare the Herb Crust:**
   - In a small bowl, combine the panko breadcrumbs, chopped parsley, chopped dill, minced garlic, and lemon zest. Mix well. Season with a small amount of salt and pepper, to taste.
3. **Season the Salmon:**
   - Pat the salmon fillets dry with a paper towel. Brush each fillet lightly with olive

oil, then spread a thin layer of Dijon mustard over the top of each fillet. This will help the herb crust adhere to the salmon and add a layer of flavor.

4. **Crust the Salmon:**
   - Press the herb and breadcrumb mixture onto the top of each salmon fillet, ensuring an even coating. The mustard will help the mixture stick to the salmon.
5. **Prepare the Asparagus:**
   - Arrange the trimmed asparagus spears on the prepared baking sheet. Drizzle with olive oil and lemon juice, and season with a small amount of salt and pepper. Toss to coat evenly.
6. **Bake the Salmon and Asparagus:**
   - Arrange the salmon fillets on the baking sheet alongside the asparagus. Bake in the preheated oven for 15-20 minutes, or until the salmon is cooked through and the herb crust is golden brown. The asparagus should be tender-crisp.
7. **Serve:**
   - Remove the salmon and asparagus from the oven. Leave the salmon to rest for a few minutes before serving. Garnish with extra lemon zest if desired. Serve the herb-crusted salmon alongside the roasted asparagus, and enjoy!

Nutritional Values (Per Serving)

- **Calories:** 350
- **Protein:** 28g
- **Carbohydrates:** 10g
- **Fat:** 23g
- **Sodium:** 180mg
- **Potassium:** 800mg
- **Phosphorus:** 350mg
- **Omega-3 Fatty Acids:** 1.5g

Note: Nutritional values are approximate and can vary based on specific ingredient brands and quantities used.

Cooking Tips

- **Choose Fresh Salmon:** For the best flavor and texture, choose fresh salmon fillets. Wild-caught salmon is generally preferred for its higher omega-3 content and cleaner taste, but farmed salmon can also be used.
- **Watch the Cooking Time:** Salmon can overcook quickly, so keep an eye on it while it's in the oven. It should be just opaque in the center and flake easily with a fork. The internal temperature should reach 145°F (63°C) when

measured with a meat thermometer.

- **Customize the Herb Mix:** Feel free to experiment with other herbs in the crust. Basil, tarragon, or chives can add different flavor profiles. If fresh herbs aren't available, dried herbs can be substituted, though you should use about half the amount since dried herbs are more concentrated.
- **Add More Vegetables:** You can add other kidney-friendly vegetables to the baking sheet, such as cherry tomatoes or sliced zucchini, for more variety and nutrients.
- **Make It Ahead:** You can prepare the herb crust and season the salmon ahead of time, then store it in the refrigerator until you're ready to bake. This makes for an easy, quick meal when you're short on time.

Health Benefits

- **Rich in Omega-3 Fatty Acids:** Salmon is one of the best sources of omega-3 fatty acids, which are essential for heart health. Omega-3s help reduce inflammation, lower blood pressure, and decrease the risk of heart disease, making them particularly beneficial for individuals on dialysis or those with cardiovascular concerns.
- **High in Protein:** This dish is high in protein, providing essential amino acids necessary for muscle repair and maintenance. Protein is especially important for individuals on dialysis, as it helps replace protein lost during the treatment process.
- **Low in Sodium:** By using fresh herbs and lemon for flavor, this recipe minimizes the need for added salt, making it a great option for those who need to monitor their sodium intake. Keeping sodium low helps reduce fluid retention and supports kidney health.
- **Rich in Antioxidants:** Asparagus is packed with vitamins A, C, and E, as well as antioxidants that help protect cells from damage. These nutrients support overall health, including immune function and skin health.
- **Supports Bone Health:** Salmon is an excellent source of vitamin D, which helps your body absorb calcium and maintain strong bones. Asparagus also contains vitamin K, which plays a role in bone health and blood clotting.
- **Aids in Weight Management:** This dish is high in protein and healthy fats, which promote satiety and can help with weight management by keeping you full longer. The fiber content in asparagus further supports digestive health and helps control appetite.

16. Turkey Meatballs with Zucchini Noodles

Preparation Time

- **15 minutes**

Cooking Time

- **25 minutes**

Serving Unit

- **4 servings**

Ingredients

For the Turkey Meatballs:

- **1 pound ground turkey** (preferably lean, 93% lean/7% fat)
- **1/4 cup breadcrumbs** (use whole wheat for added fiber)
- **1/4 cup grated Parmesan cheese** (optional, for added flavor)
- **1 large egg**, lightly beaten
- **2 cloves garlic**, minced
- **1 tablespoon fresh parsley**, chopped
- **1 tablespoon fresh basil**, chopped (or 1 teaspoon dried basil)
- **1/2 teaspoon onion powder**
- **Salt and pepper** to taste (use sparingly to keep sodium low)
- **1 tablespoon olive oil** for cooking

For the Zucchini Noodles:

- **4 medium zucchini**, spiralized into noodles (zoodles)
- **1 tablespoon olive oil**
- **1 clove garlic**, minced
- **Salt and pepper** to taste (optional)

For the Sauce:

- **2 cups marinara sauce** (low-sodium, kidney-friendly variety)
- **1/4 teaspoon red pepper flakes** (optional, for a bit of heat)

- **Fresh basil** for garnish (optional)

Procedures of Preparation

1. **Prepare the Meatball Mixture:**
    - In a large mixing bowl, combine the ground turkey, breadcrumbs, Parmesan cheese (if using), beaten egg, minced garlic, chopped parsley, chopped basil, onion powder, salt, and pepper. Mix vigorously until all of the ingredients are thoroughly combined. Avoid excessive mixing of the meatballs, since this might cause them to become tough.
2. **Form the Meatballs:**
    - With clean hands or a small ice cream scoop, form the turkey mixture into small meatballs, about 1 to 1.5 inches in diameter. This recipe should yield approximately 16-20 meatballs, depending on the size.
3. **Cook the Meatballs:**
    - In a large pan over medium heat, warm 1 tablespoon of olive oil. Once the oil is hot, add the meatballs in a single layer, ensuring they don't touch each other. Cook the meatballs for 4-5 minutes per side, turning them gently with tongs, until they are browned on all sides and cooked through. The internal temperature should reach 165°F (74°C). Take the meatballs out of the skillet and lay them aside on a plate.
4. **Prepare the Zucchini Noodles:**
    - In the same skillet, put 1 tablespoon of olive oil and garlic. Sauté the garlic for 1-2 minutes until fragrant, being careful not to burn it. Add the spiralized zucchini noodles to the skillet and toss them in the garlic oil. Cook the noodles for 3-4 minutes until they are slightly tender but still have a bit of crunch (al dente). Season with salt and pepper to taste, if desired.
5. **Heat the Marinara Sauce:**
    - In a small saucepan, heat the marinara sauce over medium-low heat. If you like a bit of heat, add the red pepper flakes to the sauce. Simmer for 5-7 minutes until the sauce is heated through.
6. **Combine and Serve:**
    - Add the cooked turkey meatballs back to the skillet with the zucchini noodles. Pour the warm

marinara sauce over the meatballs and noodles, gently tossing everything together to coat evenly.
  - Serve the turkey meatballs over a bed of zucchini noodles, garnished with fresh basil if desired.

Nutritional Values (Per Serving)

- **Calories:** 310
- **Protein:** 28g
- **Carbohydrates:** 12g
- **Fat:** 18g
- **Sodium:** 340mg
- **Potassium:** 900mg
- **Fiber:** 3g

Note: Nutritional values are approximate and can vary based on specific ingredient brands and quantities used.

Cooking Tips

- **Spiralizing Zucchini:** If you don't have a spiralizer, you can use a julienne peeler or a mandoline to create thin strips of zucchini that resemble noodles. Alternatively, many grocery stores now sell pre-spiralized zucchini in the produce section.
- **Make Ahead:** You can prepare the turkey meatballs ahead of time and store them in the refrigerator for up to 3 days or freeze them for up to 3 months. Simply reheat them with marinara sauce before serving.
- **Customize the Flavor:** Feel free to experiment with different herbs and spices in the meatballs, such as oregano, thyme, or smoked paprika, to suit your taste preferences. Adding finely chopped onions or bell peppers to the meatball mixture can also enhance the flavor.
- **Adjust the Sauce:** If you prefer a creamier sauce, you can stir in a tablespoon of Greek yogurt or a splash of cream to the marinara sauce before serving. Just be mindful of the added calories and fat content.
- **Serving Suggestions:** This dish pairs well with a simple side salad or roasted vegetables. For an added crunch, top the dish with a sprinkle of toasted pine nuts or sunflower seeds.

Health Benefits

- **Lean Protein Source:** Turkey is a lean source of high-quality protein, providing essential amino acids needed for muscle repair, immune function, and overall health. This is particularly important for individuals on dialysis who need to maintain muscle mass.
- **Low in Carbohydrates:** By using zucchini noodles instead of traditional pasta, this dish is low

in carbohydrates, making it a great option for those managing blood sugar levels or following a low-carb diet. Zucchini is also low in calories, helping with weight management.

- **Rich in Vitamins and Minerals:** Zucchini is packed with vitamins A, C, and K, as well as potassium and magnesium. These nutrients support heart health, bone health, and immune function. The potassium in zucchini also helps balance sodium levels in the body, which is beneficial for kidney health.
- **Supports Heart Health:** Turkey is low in saturated fat, making it a heart-healthy protein choice. The inclusion of olive oil and the use of low-sodium marinara sauce further support cardiovascular health by reducing cholesterol and blood pressure.
- **Antioxidant Properties:** The fresh herbs and garlic in this recipe provide antioxidants that help protect the body from oxidative stress, reducing inflammation and the risk of chronic diseases.
- **Promotes Digestive Health:** Zucchini noodles are high in fiber, which aids in digestion and helps maintain a healthy gut. Fiber also improves satiety, which helps you feel fuller for longer and aids with weight control.

17. Stuffed Bell Peppers with Brown Rice

Preparation Time

- **20 minutes**

Cooking Time

- **40 minutes**

Serving Unit

- **4 servings**

Ingredients

For the Stuffed Bell Peppers:

- **4 large bell peppers** (any color, with tops cut off and seeds removed)
- **1 cup cooked brown rice**
- **1/2 pound lean ground turkey** (or ground chicken)
- **1 medium onion**, finely chopped
- **2 cloves garlic**, minced
- **1 medium carrot**, grated
- **1 medium zucchini**, grated
- **1/2 cup canned low-sodium tomato sauce**
- **1/4 cup shredded mozzarella cheese** (optional, for topping)
- **1 tablespoon olive oil**
- **1 teaspoon dried oregano**
- **1 teaspoon dried basil**
- **Salt and pepper** to taste (use sparingly)

For the Tomato Sauce:

- **1 cup canned low-sodium tomato sauce**
- **1/4 cup water**
- **1 teaspoon dried oregano**
- **1 teaspoon dried basil**
- **Salt and pepper** to taste (optional)

Procedures of Preparation

1. **Prepare the Bell Peppers:**
    - Preheat your oven to 375°F (190°C). Cut off the tops of

the bell peppers then remove the membranes and seeds. If the peppers do not stand upright, you can trim the bottoms slightly to create a flat surface. Place the bell peppers in a baking dish, standing upright.

2. **Cook the Brown Rice:**
   - If you haven't already cooked the brown rice, do so according to the package instructions. One cup of uncooked brown rice typically yields about 2-3 cups of cooked rice. Set aside 1 cup of the cooked rice for this recipe.
3. **Prepare the Filling:**
   - In a large skillet, warm 1 tablespoon olive oil over medium heat. Add the chopped onion and simmer for 3-4 minutes, or until tender. Add the minced garlic and simmer for another 1-2 minutes, or until fragrant.
   - Add the ground turkey to the skillet and cook, breaking it up with a spoon, until it is browned and cooked through, about 5-7 minutes.
   - Stir in the grated carrot and zucchini, cooking for an additional 2-3 minutes until the vegetables are softened.
   - Add the cooked brown rice, 1/2 cup of tomato sauce, dried oregano, dried basil, salt, and pepper. Stir to combine all the ingredients, and cook for 2-3 minutes until the mixture is heated through.
4. **Stuff the Peppers:**
   - Spoon the turkey and rice mixture into each bell pepper, filling them to the top. If desired, sprinkle a small amount of shredded mozzarella cheese on top of each stuffed pepper.
5. **Prepare the Tomato Sauce:**
   - In a small bowl, mix the remaining 1 cup of tomato sauce with 1/4 cup of water, dried oregano, dried basil, salt, and pepper. Pour this sauce over and around the stuffed peppers in the baking dish.
6. **Bake the Peppers:**
   - Cover the baking dish with aluminum foil and bake the stuffed peppers in the preheated oven for 30 minutes. After 30 minutes, remove the foil and bake for an additional 10 minutes, or until the peppers are tender and the cheese (if used) is melted and golden brown.
7. **Serve:**
   - Remove the filled peppers from the oven and let them cool slightly before

serving. Spoon some of the tomato sauce from the baking dish over each stuffed pepper before serving.

Nutritional Values (Per Serving)

- **Calories:** 280
- **Protein:** 18g
- **Carbohydrates:** 30g
- **Fat:** 10g
- **Sodium:** 320mg
- **Potassium:** 850mg
- **Fiber:** 6g

Note: Nutritional values are approximate and can vary based on specific ingredient brands and quantities used.

Cooking Tips

- **Bell Pepper Variety:** You can use any color of bell pepper for this recipe, but red, yellow, and orange peppers tend to be sweeter and milder in flavor than green peppers. To get the finest results, use firm, unblemished peppers.
- **Make it Vegetarian:** If you prefer a vegetarian option, you can omit the ground turkey and replace it with additional vegetables, such as mushrooms, or use a plant-based protein like tofu or tempeh.
- **Add Extra Flavor:** For added depth of flavor, you can mix in a handful of fresh chopped herbs like parsley, cilantro, or dill into the filling. A sprinkle of crushed red pepper flakes can also add a touch of heat if desired.
- **Make Ahead:** These stuffed peppers can be assembled ahead of time and stored in the refrigerator for up to 24 hours before baking. You can also freeze the stuffed, uncooked peppers for up to 3 months. When ready to bake, simply thaw overnight in the refrigerator and bake as directed.
- **Serving Suggestions:** Serve these stuffed bell peppers with a side of steamed green beans, a simple salad, or a slice of whole-grain bread to complete the meal.

Health Benefits

- **Rich in Fiber:** Brown rice and vegetables in this recipe provide a good amount of dietary fiber, which supports digestive health, helps maintain stable blood sugar levels, and promotes satiety.
- **Lean Protein Source:** Ground turkey is a lean source of protein, which is essential for muscle repair and overall health. Protein is particularly important for individuals on dialysis, as it helps to maintain muscle mass and support immune function.

- **Low in Sodium:** This recipe uses low-sodium tomato sauce and limits added salt, making it a heart-healthy option that's suitable for those managing kidney health or hypertension.
- **High in Vitamins and Antioxidants:** Bell peppers are packed with vitamins A and C, which are powerful antioxidants that support immune function, skin health, and eye health. The additional vegetables, like carrots and zucchini, add to the vitamin and mineral content, providing a well-rounded nutrient profile.
- **Supports Heart Health:** The use of olive oil in this recipe provides healthy monounsaturated fats, which have been shown to support heart health by lowering bad cholesterol levels and reducing inflammation.
- **Kidney-Friendly:** The combination of lean protein, whole grains, and vegetables makes this dish a kidney-friendly option, providing essential nutrients without overloading on phosphorus or potassium. It's a balanced meal that can fit well into a renal diet when portion sizes are managed appropriately.

18. Lemon Garlic Shrimp with Green Beans

Preparation Time

- **10 minutes**

Cooking Time

- **15 minutes**

Serving Unit

- **4 servings**

Ingredients

- **1 pound large shrimp**, peeled and deveined
- **1 pound fresh green beans**, trimmed
- **3 tablespoons olive oil**
- **3 cloves garlic**, minced
- **Juice and zest of 1 lemon**
- **1/4 teaspoon crushed red pepper flakes** (optional, for a touch of heat)
- **1/4 teaspoon black pepper**
- **Salt to taste** (use sparingly)
- **1 tablespoon of freshly chopped parsley (optional for garnish)**

Procedures of Preparation

1. **Prepare the Shrimp:**
    - Begin by peeling and deveining the shrimp if they aren't already prepared. Rinse the shrimp in cold water and wipe dry with paper towels. Set aside.
2. **Blanch the Green Beans:**
    - In a large pot, bring water to a boil. Add a pinch of salt if desired. Add the trimmed green beans and cook them for about 3-4 minutes until they are tender-crisp. Drain the beans and immediately transfer them to a bowl of

ice water to stop the cooking process and maintain their vibrant green color. Once cooled, drain the beans and set them aside.

3. **Cook the Shrimp:**
   - In a large pan, heat 2 tablespoons of olive oil over medium heat. Add the minced garlic and sauté for about 1 minute until fragrant, being careful not to burn the garlic.
   - Add the shrimp to the skillet in one layer. Cook the shrimp for approximately 2 minutes on each side, until they are pink and opaque. Be careful not to overcook the shrimp, as they may turn tough and rubbery.
4. **Combine the Ingredients:**
   - Add the blanched green beans to the skillet with the shrimp. Pour in the remaining tablespoon of olive oil, lemon juice, lemon zest, crushed red pepper flakes (if using), black pepper, and a small amount of salt. Toss everything together in the skillet, cooking for an additional 2-3 minutes until the green beans are heated through and coated in the lemon garlic sauce.
5. **Serve:**
   - Remove the skillet from heat. Garnish the dish with chopped fresh parsley if desired. Serve immediately, either as a stand-alone dish or over a bed of steamed rice or quinoa.

Nutritional Values (Per Serving)

- **Calories:** 210
- **Protein:** 22g
- **Carbohydrates:** 8g
- **Fat:** 12g
- **Sodium:** 310mg
- **Potassium:** 410mg
- **Fiber:** 3g

Note: Nutritional values are approximate and can vary based on specific ingredient brands and quantities used.

Cooking Tips

- **Choosing Shrimp:** For the best flavor, choose large, fresh shrimp if possible. If using frozen shrimp, be sure to let them defrost completely before cooking. You can quickly thaw shrimp by placing them in a colander under cold running water for several minutes.
- **Adjusting the Spice:** If you enjoy a bit of heat, the crushed red pepper flakes add a nice kick

to the dish. However, if you prefer a milder flavor, you can omit them entirely.

- **Lemon Variations:** The lemon juice and zest are key to this dish's fresh, zesty flavor. For an extra lemony punch, you can add more zest or squeeze a little extra lemon juice over the finished dish.
- **Adding Vegetables:** If you want to add more variety, consider incorporating other quick-cooking vegetables like cherry tomatoes, bell peppers, or asparagus along with the green beans.
- **Serving Suggestions:** This dish pairs well with a side of whole grains, such as brown rice or quinoa, or with a simple salad. You can also serve it with whole-grain pasta for a more substantial meal.
- **Make It a One-Pan Meal:** If you prefer, you can cook the shrimp and green beans together in the same skillet from the start. Just be sure to adjust the cooking times so that the shrimp don't overcook.

Health Benefits

- **High in Protein:** Shrimp is an excellent source of lean protein, which is essential for maintaining muscle mass and supporting overall body function. Protein is especially important for individuals on dialysis, as it helps repair tissues and supports immune health.
- **Low in Fat:** This dish is low in saturated fat, making it a heart-healthy option. The use of olive oil, rich in monounsaturated fats, supports heart health by helping to reduce bad cholesterol levels.
- **Rich in Antioxidants:** Garlic and lemon are both rich in antioxidants, which help protect the body from oxidative stress and inflammation. Antioxidants are essential for preserving general health and avoiding chronic illnesses.
- **Kidney-Friendly:** This recipe is low in sodium, making it suitable for those managing kidney health or hypertension. The shrimp and green beans provide essential nutrients without overloading on potassium or phosphorus.
- **Boosts Immunity:** The vitamin C in lemon juice and the allicin in garlic are known for their immune-boosting properties. These ingredients help support the body's defense system, which is especially important for individuals with compromised kidney function.
- **Supports Digestive Health:** Green beans are a good source of dietary fiber, which aids in digestion and helps maintain a healthy gut. Fiber also plays a role in controlling blood sugar levels and supporting heart health.

19. Baked Chicken Breasts with Cauliflower Rice

Preparation Time

- **15 minutes**

Cooking Time

- **30 minutes**

Serving Unit

- **4 servings**

Ingredients

- **4 boneless, skinless chicken breasts** (about 6 ounces each)
- **1 medium head of cauliflower**, grated or processed into rice-sized pieces
- **3 tablespoons olive oil**
- **3 cloves garlic**, minced
- **1 teaspoon paprika**
- **1 teaspoon dried thyme**
- **1 teaspoon dried oregano**
- **1/2 teaspoon black pepper**
- **Salt to taste** (use sparingly)
- **Juice of 1 lemon**
- **1/4 cup low-sodium chicken broth**
- **Fresh parsley**, chopped (for garnish)

Procedures of Preparation

1. **Preheat the Oven:**
   - Preheat your oven to 375°F (190°C). While the oven heats up, prepare the chicken and cauliflower rice.
2. **Prepare the Chicken Breasts:**
   - In a small bowl, mix together 2 tablespoons of olive oil, paprika, thyme, oregano, black pepper, and a small amount of salt.
   - Brush the chicken breasts on both sides with this seasoned olive oil mixture. Make sure each breast is evenly coated to ensure

they bake with a flavorful crust.

3. **Bake the Chicken:**
    - Put the seasoned chicken breasts in a baking tray. Pour the low-sodium chicken broth into the dish to keep the chicken moist as it bakes.
    - Cover the baking dish with aluminum foil and bake the chicken in the preheated oven for about 25-30 minutes, or until the internal temperature of the chicken reaches 165°F (75°C).
    - For a golden-brown finish, remove the foil during the last 5 minutes of baking. When done, take the chicken from the oven and allow it to rest for 5 minutes before serving.
4. **Prepare the Cauliflower Rice:**
    - While the chicken is baking, heat the remaining tablespoon of olive oil in a large skillet over medium heat.
    - Sauté the minced garlic for approximately a minute, or until fragrant. Be cautious not to burn the garlic.
    - Add the grated cauliflower to the skillet and stir to combine with the garlic. Cook the cauliflower rice for 5–7 minutes, stirring periodically, until soft but not mushy.
    - Squeeze the lemon juice over the cauliflower rice, and season with a small amount of salt and black pepper to taste.
5. **Serve:**
    - To serve, place a portion of the cauliflower rice on each plate. Top with a baked chicken breast and garnish with freshly chopped parsley. Optionally, you can drizzle a little more lemon juice over the chicken for extra flavor.

Nutritional Values (Per Serving)

- **Calories:** 280
- **Protein:** 35g
- **Carbohydrates:** 7g
- **Fat:** 12g
- **Sodium:** 180mg
- **Potassium:** 650mg
- **Fiber:** 3g

Note: Nutritional values are approximate and can vary based on specific ingredient brands and quantities used.

Cooking Tips

- **Ensure Even Cooking:** Pound the chicken breasts to an even thickness before baking to ensure they cook evenly. This also helps prevent the chicken from drying out.

- **Cauliflower Rice Consistency:** When preparing cauliflower rice, be careful not to overcook it. The goal is to have a texture similar to al dente rice—tender but with a bit of bite.
- **Flavor Variations:** You can easily change up the flavors of this dish by adding different herbs or spices to the chicken marinade. Try using rosemary, cumin, or even a dash of cayenne pepper for a different twist.
- **Low-Sodium Chicken Broth:** Using low-sodium chicken broth helps keep the sodium content in check, which is especially important for individuals managing kidney health.
- **Adding Vegetables:** Consider adding other low-potassium vegetables like bell peppers or zucchini to the cauliflower rice for added color, flavor, and nutrients.

Health Benefits

- **High in Protein:** Chicken breasts are an excellent source of lean protein, crucial for maintaining muscle mass, especially in individuals with chronic kidney disease (CKD) who may experience muscle wasting. Protein also aids in tissue repair and supports overall body functions.
- **Low in Carbohydrates:** Cauliflower rice is a fantastic low-carb alternative to traditional rice, making this dish suitable for those managing blood sugar levels or following a low-carb diet.
- **Rich in Vitamins and Minerals:** Cauliflower is rich in vitamins C and K, as well as folate and fiber. These nutrients support immune function, bone health, and digestive health, making cauliflower rice a nutritious base for the meal.
- **Supports Heart Health:** The use of olive oil, which is high in monounsaturated fats, promotes heart health by helping to lower bad cholesterol levels. The dish's overall low-fat content also makes it a heart-friendly option.
- **Kidney-Friendly:** This dish is designed to be low in sodium, which is important for managing blood pressure and kidney function. It's also low in phosphorus and potassium, making it a suitable choice for individuals on a renal diet.
- **Antioxidant Properties:** Garlic, thyme, and oregano are rich in antioxidants, which help reduce inflammation and protect cells from damage. Antioxidants play a critical role in managing chronic diseases, including CKD.
- **Weight Management:** With its high protein content and

low-calorie count, this dish is an excellent option for weight management. The protein helps increase satiety, reducing the likelihood of overeating.

20. Beef Stir-Fry with Bell Peppers

Preparation Time

- **20 minutes**

Cooking Time

- **15 minutes**

Serving Unit

- **4 servings**

Ingredients

- **1 pound (450g) of thinly sliced beef sirloin or flank steak**
- **1 red bell pepper**, thinly sliced
- **1 yellow bell pepper**, thinly sliced
- **1 green bell pepper**, thinly sliced
- **1 medium onion**, thinly sliced
- **3 cloves garlic**, minced
- **2 tablespoons low-sodium soy sauce**
- **1 tablespoon oyster sauce** (optional, can use low-sodium version)
- **1 tablespoon cornstarch**
- **1 tablespoon olive oil**
- **1 teaspoon fresh ginger**, minced
- **1/4 teaspoon black pepper**
- **1/4 cup low-sodium beef broth**
- **Fresh cilantro or green onions**, chopped (for garnish)

Procedures of Preparation

1. **Prepare the Beef:**
   - Start by slicing the beef thinly across the grain. This helps tenderize the meat, making it easier to cook and chew.
   - In a bowl, combine the sliced beef with 1 tablespoon of low-sodium soy sauce, 1 tablespoon of cornstarch, and black

pepper. Mix well until the meat is uniformly coated. Let it marinate for about 10 minutes to absorb the flavors and ensure tenderness.

2. **Prepare the Vegetables:**
   - While the beef is marinating, wash and slice the red, yellow, and green bell peppers into thin strips. Slice the onion, then mince the garlic and ginger. Set the vegetables aside.
3. **Cook the Beef:**
   - In a large pan or wok, heat 1 tablespoon of olive oil over medium to high heat. Once the oil is heated, arrange the marinated meat in a single layer. Stir-fry the beef for about 3-4 minutes until it's browned on all sides.
   - Remove the steak from the skillet and put aside.
4. **Cook the Vegetables:**
   - In the same skillet, mix the minced garlic and ginger. Stir-fry for about a minute, until aromatic.
   - Place the cut onions and bell peppers in the skillet. Stir-fry the vegetables for about 5 minutes until they are tender but still slightly crisp. The bell peppers should retain their vibrant color.
5. **Combine and Finish:**
   - Return the cooked meat to the pan and add the veggies. Stir in the remaining 1 tablespoon of low-sodium soy sauce, oyster sauce (if using), and low-sodium beef broth.
   - Stir everything together and cook for an additional 2-3 minutes until the beef is heated through and the sauce has thickened slightly.
6. **Serve:**
   - Serve the beef stir-fry over steamed brown rice, quinoa, or cauliflower rice for a low-carb option. Garnish with freshly chopped cilantro or green onions for a burst of freshness.

Nutritional Values (Per Serving)

- **Calories:** 280
- **Protein:** 25g
- **Carbohydrates:** 12g
- **Fat:** 14g
- **Sodium:** 380mg
- **Potassium:** 650mg
- **Fiber:** 3g

Note: Nutritional values are approximate and can vary based on specific ingredient brands and quantities used.

Cooking Tips

- **Thinly Slicing the Beef:** To make slicing easier, partially freeze the beef for about 30 minutes before cutting. This will firm up the meat, allowing for thinner, more even slices.
- **High Heat for Stir-Frying:** Stir-frying requires high heat to cook the ingredients quickly and evenly. Make sure your skillet or wok is very hot before adding the beef or vegetables to achieve the best results.
- **Vegetable Variations:** Feel free to add other vegetables to the stir-fry, such as broccoli, snap peas, or carrots. Just be mindful of the cooking times for each vegetable to ensure they remain crisp-tender.
- **Sauce Adjustments:** If you prefer a thicker sauce, mix an additional teaspoon of cornstarch with a little water and add it to the stir-fry at the end of cooking. Stir until the sauce thickens.
- **Low-Sodium Option:** Use low-sodium soy sauce and oyster sauce to keep the sodium content in check, especially for those managing their kidney health or blood pressure. You can also dilute the soy sauce with water if you want to reduce the sodium further.
- **Garnishing:** Adding fresh herbs like cilantro or green onions at the end not only enhances the flavor but also adds a vibrant color contrast, making the dish more visually appealing.

Health Benefits

- **High in Protein:** This dish provides a substantial amount of high-quality protein from the beef, which is essential for muscle repair and maintenance, particularly important for individuals with chronic kidney disease (CKD) who may be experiencing muscle wasting.
- **Rich in Vitamins and Antioxidants:** Bell peppers are rich in vitamins A and C, which are powerful antioxidants. These vitamins support immune function, skin health, and vision. They also help neutralize free radicals, reducing oxidative stress, which is beneficial for overall health, including kidney function.
- **Supports Heart Health:** The use of olive oil in this recipe adds heart-healthy monounsaturated fats, which can help reduce bad cholesterol levels and lower the risk of heart disease. Maintaining heart health is particularly important for individuals with kidney disease, as they are at higher risk for cardiovascular complications.
- **Low in Carbohydrates:** By serving this stir-fry with cauliflower rice or as is, you can keep the carbohydrate content

low, making it a suitable option for those managing their blood sugar levels or following a low-carb diet.

- **Kidney-Friendly:** The recipe is designed to be lower in sodium by using low-sodium soy sauce and oyster sauce, making it a suitable choice for those on a renal diet. The lower sodium content helps in managing blood pressure and reducing the risk of further kidney damage.
- **Promotes Digestive Health:** Bell peppers and onions are good sources of dietary fiber, which supports digestive health by promoting regular bowel movements and preventing constipation. A healthy digestive system is crucial for overall well-being, especially when managing chronic conditions.
- **Anti-Inflammatory Properties:** Garlic and ginger, both used in this recipe, have anti-inflammatory properties. They help reduce inflammation in the body, which is beneficial for individuals with chronic illnesses, including CKD, where inflammation often plays a role in disease progression.

21. Butternut Squash Risotto

Preparation Time

- **15 minutes**

Cooking Time

- **30 minutes**

Serving Unit

- **4 servings**

Ingredients

- **1 cup Arborio rice**
- **2 cups butternut squash**, peeled and diced
- **4 cups low-sodium vegetable broth**
- **1 small onion**, finely chopped
- **2 cloves garlic**, minced
- **1/2 cup dry white wine** (optional)
- **1/4 cup grated Parmesan cheese** (optional, for garnish)
- **2 tablespoons olive oil**
- **1 tablespoon unsalted butter**
- **1/2 teaspoon fresh thyme leaves** (optional)
- **1/4 teaspoon black pepper**
- **Fresh parsley**, chopped (for garnish)

Procedures of Preparation

1. **Prepare the Butternut Squash:**
   - Begin by peeling and dicing the butternut squash into small, bite-sized cubes. The smaller the cubes, the quicker they will cook, and they'll blend seamlessly into the risotto.
2. **Cook the Butternut Squash:**
   - Heat 1 tablespoon olive oil in a large saucepan over medium heat Add the diced butternut squash and cook, stirring occasionally, for about 5-7

    minutes until the squash starts to soften and develop a light golden color.
    - Remove the squash from the pot and set it aside.
3. **Sauté the Aromatics:**
    - In the same pot, add the remaining 1 tablespoon of olive oil and the butter. Once the butter has melted, add the chopped onion and sauté for 3-4 minutes until translucent.
    - Add the minced garlic and simmer for another minute, or until fragrant.
4. **Toast the Rice:**
    - Add the Arborio rice to the pot with the sautéed onions and garlic. Stir to coat the rice grains in the oil and butter, toasting them for 2-3 minutes until they become slightly translucent around the edges.
5. **Deglaze with Wine (Optional):**
    - Pour in the white wine (if using) and stir continuously until the wine is absorbed by the rice. This step adds a depth of flavor to the risotto.
6. **Add the Broth Gradually:**
    - Begin adding the low-sodium vegetable broth to the rice, one ladle at a time. Stir constantly and wait until the broth is absorbed before adding more. Continue cooking for about 20 minutes, or until the rice is creamy and al dente.
    - Stir in the cooked butternut squash about halfway through the broth addition, allowing the squash to break down slightly and incorporate into the risotto.
7. **Finish the Risotto:**
    - Once the risotto is creamy and the rice is fully cooked, stir in the fresh thyme leaves (if using), black pepper, and grated Parmesan cheese (if using).
    - Adjust the seasoning as needed, but be cautious with salt due to the low-sodium dietary requirements.
8. **Serve:**
    - Serve the butternut squash risotto hot, garnished with freshly chopped parsley for a pop of color and added freshness.

Nutritional Values (Per Serving)

- **Calories:** 290
- **Protein:** 6g
- **Carbohydrates:** 45g
- **Fat:** 9g

- **Sodium:** 100mg
- **Potassium:** 500mg
- **Fiber:** 4g

Note: Nutritional values are approximate and can vary based on specific ingredient brands and quantities used.

Cooking Tips

- **Choose the Right Rice:** Arborio rice is essential for achieving the creamy texture of risotto. Its high starch content is what gives risotto its signature creaminess, so avoid substituting it with other types of rice.
- **Keep the Broth Warm:** To ensure even cooking and maintain the temperature of the risotto, keep the vegetable broth warm in a separate pot while you're cooking. Adding cold broth might slow down the cooking process and change the final texture.
- **Don't Rush the Process:** Risotto requires patience. The key to a perfect risotto is gradually adding the broth and stirring frequently. This process allows the rice to release its starches, creating a creamy consistency without the need for cream.
- **Customizing Flavors:** For an extra layer of flavor, you can add a pinch of nutmeg or cinnamon to the butternut squash while it's cooking. These spices complement the natural sweetness of the squash and add warmth to the dish.
- **Vegetarian Option:** This recipe is naturally vegetarian, but to make it vegan, simply omit the Parmesan cheese and use a dairy-free butter substitute.

Health Benefits

- **Rich in Vitamins and Antioxidants:** Butternut squash is an excellent source of vitamins A and C, which are important for immune function, skin health, and vision. It also includes antioxidants, which assist the body resist oxidative stress.
- **Supports Digestive Health:** The fiber content in butternut squash and Arborio rice promotes healthy digestion. Fiber helps regulate bowel movements, supports gut health, and can help manage blood sugar levels by slowing the absorption of carbohydrates.
- **Low in Sodium:** This risotto is designed to be low in sodium, making it suitable for individuals managing their kidney health or those on a low-sodium diet. Keeping sodium intake in check is crucial for controlling blood pressure and reducing the risk of further kidney damage.
- **Balanced Carbohydrates:** Arborio rice provides a steady source of carbohydrates, which

are important for energy. The gradual release of glucose into the bloodstream helps maintain stable blood sugar levels, making this dish suitable for those with diabetes or insulin resistance.

- **Heart-Healthy Fats:** The olive oil and butter used in this recipe contribute to healthy fat intake. Olive oil contains monounsaturated fats, which may help decrease bad cholesterol and lessen the risk of heart disease.
- **Kidney-Friendly:** The use of low-sodium broth and controlled seasoning ensures that this dish is kidney-friendly, helping to manage fluid retention and prevent hypertension, common concerns for those undergoing dialysis

4

Snacks

22. Apple Slices with Almond Butter

Preparation Time

- **5 minutes**

Cooking Time

- **None**

Serving Unit

- **2 servings**

Ingredients

- **1 large apple** (such as Fuji, Gala, or Honeycrisp)
- **2 tablespoons almond butter**
- **Optional toppings:**
  - **1 teaspoon chia seeds**
  - **1 teaspoon honey (optional, depending on sweetness preference)**
  - **A pinch of cinnamon**

Procedures of Preparation

1. **Prepare the Apple:**
   - Wash the apple thoroughly under running water to remove any dirt or pesticides.
   - Core the apple and slice it into thin wedges, approximately 8-10 slices depending on the size of the apple.
2. **Plate the Apple Slices:**
   - Arrange the apple slices on a serving plate in a fan-like pattern or simply in a circular arrangement.
3. **Serve with Almond Butter:**
   - Place 2 tablespoons of almond butter in a small dish or directly on the plate for dipping.
   - If desired, drizzle a little honey over the almond butter for added sweetness, especially if the apple is more tart than sweet.

4. **Optional Toppings:**
    - Sprinkle chia seeds over the almond butter or the apple slices for an added nutritional boost.
    - Dust the apple slices with a pinch of cinnamon, which pairs well with the sweetness of the apple and the richness of the almond butter.
5. **Enjoy:**
    - Serve immediately to enjoy the fresh, crisp taste of the apples and the creamy almond butter.

Nutritional Values (Per Serving)

- **Calories:** 150
- **Protein:** 4g
- **Carbohydrates:** 20g
- **Fat:** 8g
- **Sodium:** 1mg
- **Potassium:** 200mg
- **Fiber:** 4g

Note: Nutritional values are approximate and can vary based on specific ingredient brands and quantities used.

Cooking Tips

- **Choosing the Right Apple:** Select an apple variety that suits your taste preference. Fuji and Honeycrisp are great for their sweetness and crisp texture, while Granny Smith offers a tart contrast that pairs well with the creaminess of almond butter.
- **Almond Butter Consistency:** If your almond butter is too thick, you can mix in a small amount of warm water or milk to thin it out slightly, making it easier to dip the apple slices.
- **Toppings Variations:** Feel free to experiment with different toppings. Flaxseeds, crushed nuts, or even a sprinkle of cocoa powder can add variety to this simple snack.
- **Storage Tips:** If you're preparing this snack to eat later, store the apple slices in a resealable plastic bag with a few drops of lemon juice to prevent browning. Keep the almond butter in a separate container.
- **Make It a Mini Meal:** To turn this snack into a more substantial mini meal, consider adding a handful of whole-grain crackers or a piece of low-sodium cheese on the side.

Health Benefits

- **Rich in Fiber:** Apples are an excellent source of dietary fiber, which supports healthy digestion by promoting regular bowel movements. Fiber also helps manage blood sugar levels, making this snack a good choice for individuals with diabetes or those looking to maintain stable energy levels throughout the day.

- **Heart-Healthy Fats:** Almond butter is rich in monounsaturated fats, which are beneficial for heart health. These fats can help lower bad cholesterol levels and reduce the risk of heart disease, making this snack a heart-friendly option.
- **Kidney-Friendly:** Both apples and almond butter are low in sodium and potassium, making this snack suitable for individuals on a renal diet. The low sodium content helps manage blood pressure, and the moderate potassium levels support kidney function without overloading the kidneys.
- **Antioxidant-Rich:** Apples contain antioxidants, such as vitamin C and flavonoids, which help protect the body from oxidative stress. This is particularly important for individuals with chronic conditions, including kidney disease, where oxidative stress can exacerbate health issues.
- **Energy Boosting:** The combination of natural sugars from the apple and healthy fats from the almond butter provides a quick and sustained energy boost, making it an ideal snack for any time of day. The natural sugars provide immediate energy, while the fats ensure a slow release, keeping you full and energized for longer.
- **Supports Weight Management:** The fiber in apples and the protein in almond butter work together to promote satiety, helping you feel fuller for longer. This can be beneficial for weight management, as it may reduce the urge to snack on less healthy options between meals.

23. Carrot Sticks with Hummus

Preparation Time

- **10 minutes**

Cooking Time

- **None**

Serving Unit

- **2 servings**

Ingredients

- **4 large carrots**
- **½ cup hummus** (store-bought or homemade)
- **Optional garnishes:**
  - **A sprinkle of paprika**
  - **A drizzle of olive oil**
  - **Chopped parsley**

Procedures of Preparation

1. **Prepare the Carrots:**
   - Wash the carrots very well with running water to eliminate any dirt or debris.
   - Peel the carrots if desired, though leaving the peel on can add extra fiber and nutrients.
   - Cut the carrots into sticks, approximately 3-4 inches long and about ½ inch thick. Ensure that the sticks are uniform in size for consistent texture and ease of eating.
2. **Prepare the Hummus:**
   - If using store-bought hummus, simply spoon it into a serving bowl.
   - For an extra touch, garnish the hummus with a sprinkle of paprika, a drizzle of olive oil, and some chopped parsley.
3. **Serve:**

   - Arrange the carrot sticks on a serving plate around the hummus bowl or in a separate section.
   - Serve immediately to enjoy the fresh, crisp carrots paired with the creamy hummus.
4. **Storage:**
   - If you're preparing this snack in advance, store the carrot sticks in a resealable plastic bag in the refrigerator, and keep the hummus in a separate airtight container.

Nutritional Values (Per Serving)

- **Calories:** 120
- **Protein:** 3g
- **Carbohydrates:** 16g
- **Fat:** 5g
- **Sodium:** 150mg (varies based on hummus)
- **Potassium:** 400mg
- **Fiber:** 5g

Note: Nutritional values are approximate and can vary based on specific ingredient brands and quantities used.

Cooking Tips

- **Hummus Variations:** To add some variety, try different flavors of hummus such as roasted red pepper, garlic, or even avocado hummus. Each variation will bring a unique flavor profile to the dish.
- **Carrot Sticks Alternative:** If you're looking to mix things up, try using other vegetables like cucumber sticks, bell pepper strips, or celery sticks as a substitute or in addition to the carrots.
- **Homemade Hummus:** If you have a bit more time, making your own hummus can elevate the dish. Simply blend cooked chickpeas, tahini, olive oil, lemon juice, garlic, and salt in a food processor until smooth. Adjust seasoning to taste.
- **Spicing it Up:** For those who enjoy a bit of heat, adding a pinch of cayenne pepper or red pepper flakes to the hummus can give it an extra kick.
- **Texture Preference:** For a creamier hummus, add more olive oil or a bit of water while blending. If you prefer it thicker, reduce the amount of liquid or add more chickpeas.

Health Benefits

- **Rich in Beta-Carotene:** Carrots are an excellent source of beta-carotene, a powerful antioxidant that the body converts into vitamin A. This vitamin is crucial for keeping clear eyesight, a robust immune system, and healthy skin.

- **Heart-Healthy Snack:** Hummus is made primarily from chickpeas, which are rich in fiber and plant-based protein. These nutrients contribute to heart health by helping to lower cholesterol levels and stabilize blood sugar.
- **Supports Digestive Health:** The fiber in both carrots and hummus aids in digestion by promoting regular bowel movements and feeding the beneficial bacteria in your gut. A diet rich in fiber can help prevent constipation and reduce the risk of colon cancer.
- **Low in Calories, High in Nutrients:** This snack is low in calories but packed with essential nutrients like potassium, which helps regulate blood pressure, and vitamin K, which is important for bone health.
- **Kidney-Friendly Option:** Carrots are naturally low in sodium and potassium, making them a great option for individuals following a renal diet. Hummus can also be kidney-friendly when consumed in moderation, as it is low in saturated fat and provides plant-based protein.
- **Promotes Satiety:** The combination of fiber and protein in this snack helps promote satiety, making you feel fuller for longer. This may be very useful for weight management and avoiding overeating.
- **Anti-Inflammatory Properties:** Both carrots and hummus contain nutrients that have anti-inflammatory properties. Carrots are rich in antioxidants, while the garlic and olive oil in hummus contribute to reducing inflammation in the body, which is crucial for managing chronic conditions like arthritis and heart disease.

24. Cottage Cheese with Cucumber

Preparation Time

- **5 minutes**

Cooking Time

- **None**

Serving Unit

- **2 servings**

Ingredients

- **1 cup low-sodium cottage cheese**
- **1 medium cucumber**
- **1 tablespoon fresh dill, chopped** (optional)
- **1 tablespoon olive oil** (optional)
- **Freshly ground black pepper to taste**

Procedures of Preparation

1. **Prepare the Cucumber:**
   - Wash the cucumber thoroughly under cold running water.
   - Peel the cucumber if desired, or leave the skin on for added texture and nutrients.
   - Slice the cucumber into thin rounds or small cubes, depending on your preference.
2. **Combine the Ingredients:**
   - In a medium-sized mixing bowl, add the cottage cheese.
   - Gently fold in the cucumber slices or cubes.
   - If you're using dill, add it to the mixture for an extra layer of flavor.
3. **Season and Serve:**

- Drizzle the olive oil over the top for added richness, if desired.
- Add freshly ground black pepper to taste.
- Serve immediately as a side dish or refreshing snack.

4. **Storage:**
    - If there are any leftovers, keep them in an airtight container and store them in the refrigerator. Consume within 1-2 days to ensure maximum freshness.

Nutritional Values (Per Serving)

- **Calories:** 90
- **Protein:** 12g
- **Carbohydrates:** 4g
- **Fat:** 3g
- **Sodium:** 180mg (may vary based on cottage cheese used)
- **Potassium:** 200mg
- **Calcium:** 100mg

Note: Nutritional values are approximate and can vary based on specific ingredient brands and quantities used.

Cooking Tips

- **Cucumber Variations:** English cucumbers or Persian cucumbers are great options for this dish because they have fewer seeds and a milder flavor. You can also try different varieties to see which you prefer.
- **Herb Substitutes:** If dill isn't your favorite, consider using other fresh herbs like parsley, chives, or mint. Each herb will provide a unique flavor twist.
- **Texture Preferences:** Cottage cheese comes in different curd sizes—small, medium, and large. Choose the one that best suits your texture preferences. For a smoother consistency, you can even blend the cottage cheese before adding the cucumber.
- **Additional Vegetables:** For a more colorful and nutrient-rich dish, you can add other vegetables like cherry tomatoes, bell peppers, or radishes.
- **Flavor Enhancements:** A squeeze of fresh lemon juice can brighten the dish, while a pinch of garlic powder can add a bit of depth. Experiment with these additions until you discover the ideal mix.

Health Benefits

- **Rich in Protein:** Cottage cheese is an excellent source of high-quality protein, which is essential for maintaining muscle mass and overall health, especially for individuals with kidney concerns who need to monitor their protein intake carefully.

- **Low in Calories:** This dish is low in calories, making it a great option for those who are watching their weight or managing calorie intake for health reasons.
- **Supports Bone Health:** Cottage cheese is rich in calcium, which is vital for maintaining strong bones and teeth. Regular consumption of calcium-rich foods can help reduce the risk of osteoporosis.
- **Hydrating and Low in Sodium:** Cucumbers are composed of about 95% water, making them incredibly hydrating. They are also naturally low in sodium, which is beneficial for those on a renal diet who need to limit their sodium intake.
- **Antioxidant Properties:** Cucumbers contain antioxidants like beta-carotene and flavonoids, which help protect your body from damage caused by free radicals.
- **Digestive Health:** Cucumbers include fiber, which assists digestion and may prevent constipation. Additionally, the probiotics found in some cottage cheese varieties support gut health by promoting a healthy balance of bacteria in the digestive system.
- **Kidney-Friendly:** This recipe is designed to be low in sodium and potassium, making it suitable for individuals with kidney concerns. However, portion control is important to ensure the dish fits within your dietary needs.
- **Heart Health:** The combination of low-fat cottage cheese and fresh cucumber provides a heart-healthy dish that's low in saturated fat. The optional olive oil adds monounsaturated fats, which are beneficial for heart health.

25. Rice Cakes with Avocado

Preparation Time

- **5 minutes**

Cooking Time

- **None**

Serving Unit

- **2 servings**

Ingredients

- **2 whole-grain rice cakes**
- **1 ripe avocado**
- **1 teaspoon lemon juice**
- **Pinch of sea salt** (optional, based on dietary needs)
- **Freshly ground black pepper to taste**
- **Optional toppings:** Sliced cherry tomatoes, radishes, or sprouts

---

Procedures of Preparation

1. **Prepare the Avocado:**
   - Cut a ripe avocado in half and take out the pit.
   - Scrape the avocado flesh into a small bowl.
   - Add the lemon juice to the avocado to prevent browning and enhance flavor.
   - Mash the avocado with a fork until smooth or leave it slightly chunky, depending on your preference.
2. **Assemble the Rice Cakes:**
   - Place the whole-grain rice cakes on a plate.
   - Spread an even layer of the mashed avocado on each rice cake.
3. **Season and Garnish:**
   - Sprinkle a pinch of sea salt and freshly ground black pepper over the avocado, if desired.

   - Add any optional toppings like sliced cherry tomatoes, radishes, or sprouts to enhance the flavor and nutritional value.
4. **Serve Immediately:**
   - Enjoy the rice cakes with avocado as a quick snack, breakfast, or light lunch.

Nutritional Values (Per Serving)

- **Calories:** 150
- **Protein:** 3g
- **Carbohydrates:** 18g
- **Fat:** 9g
- **Sodium:** 50mg (varies based on added salt and type of rice cakes)
- **Potassium:** 370mg
- **Fiber:** 5g

Note: Nutritional values are approximate and can vary based on specific ingredient brands and quantities used.

Cooking Tips

- **Choosing the Right Avocado:** Make sure to use a ripe avocado for the best flavor and texture. A ripe avocado will yield slightly when gently pressed but shouldn't be too soft.
- **Rice Cake Selection:** Opt for whole-grain or brown rice cakes, as they provide more fiber and nutrients compared to refined rice cakes. You can also experiment with different flavors, such as lightly salted or sesame, to complement the avocado.
- **Customizing Toppings:** Feel free to customize your rice cakes with a variety of toppings. Cherry tomatoes add a burst of sweetness, while radishes provide a crisp texture. Sprouts, such as alfalfa or broccoli sprouts, can add a fresh and earthy flavor.
- **Portion Control:** Although avocados are nutritious, they are high in calories. Be mindful of portion sizes to maintain a balanced diet, especially if you are managing your calorie intake.
- **Storage Tips:** If you have leftover avocado, store it in an airtight container with a bit of lemon juice to prevent browning. Consume within a day or two for optimal quality.

Health Benefits

- **Rich in Healthy Fats:** Avocados are an excellent source of monounsaturated fats, which are heart-healthy and can help lower bad cholesterol levels. These fats also assist in the absorption of fat-soluble vitamins A, D, E, and K.
- **High in Fiber:** Both the rice cakes and avocado contribute to the fiber content of this dish. Fiber is essential for digestive

health, helping to prevent constipation and maintain a healthy gut. It also supports blood sugar control and can aid in weight management by promoting a feeling of fullness.

- **Potassium Boost:** Avocados are rich in potassium, an essential mineral that helps regulate blood pressure, balance fluids, and support muscle function. For individuals with kidney concerns, it's important to monitor potassium intake, so adjust the portion size accordingly.
- **Low in Sodium:** This recipe can be made with minimal or no added salt, making it suitable for those following a low-sodium diet. Reducing sodium intake is crucial for managing blood pressure and reducing the risk of heart disease, particularly for individuals with kidney issues.
- **Antioxidant Properties:** Avocados are packed with antioxidants like vitamin E and C, which help protect the body from oxidative stress and inflammation. These antioxidants may improve general health and perhaps lower the risk of chronic illnesses.
- **Supports Weight Management:** The combination of healthy fats and fiber in avocados can promote satiety, helping to curb overeating and support weight management goals.
- **Kidney-Friendly Option:** By using low-sodium rice cakes and controlling the portion of avocado, this dish can be a kidney-friendly snack that fits into a renal diet. The balance of healthy fats, fiber, and low sodium content makes it a nutritious choice for those managing kidney health.
- **Versatile and Satisfying:** This recipe is versatile enough to be enjoyed at any time of the day. It's a satisfying snack that provides a balance of macronutrients, making it a great option for maintaining energy levels throughout the day.

26. Mixed Nuts and Dried Fruits

Preparation Time

- **5 minutes**

Cooking Time

- **None**

Serving Unit

- **4 servings**

Ingredients

- **1/4 cup almonds**
- **1/4 cup walnuts**
- **1/4 cup cashews**
- **1/4 cup pistachios**
- **1/4 cup dried apricots (unsweetened)**
- **1/4 cup raisins**
- **1/4 cup dried cranberries (unsweetened)**
- **1/4 cup dried apple slices (unsweetened)**

Note: You can customize the nuts and dried fruits based on your preferences or dietary needs.

Procedures of Preparation

1. **Prepare the Ingredients:**
    - Measure out the nuts and dried fruits into separate bowls.
    - If the dried fruits are large, like dried apricots or apple slices, chop them into bite-sized pieces for easier mixing and consumption.
2. **Mix the Ingredients:**
    - In a large bowl, combine the almonds, walnuts, cashews, and pistachios.
    - Add the chopped dried apricots, raisins, dried cranberries, and dried apple slices to the bowl.
3. **Toss to Combine:**
    - Gently toss the nuts and dried fruits together to

ensure they are evenly mixed.

4. **Store or Serve:**
   - Divide the mixture into individual servings or store it in an airtight container for later use.
   - Enjoy this mix as a snack on its own or add it to yogurt, oatmeal, or salads for extra flavor and nutrition.

Nutritional Values (Per Serving)

- **Calories:** 200-220 (varies based on specific types and quantities of nuts and dried fruits used)
- **Protein:** 5-6g
- **Carbohydrates:** 20-25g
- **Fat:** 12-15g
- **Fiber:** 3-4g
- **Sodium:** 0-10mg (naturally occurring)
- **Sugar:** 12-15g (from dried fruits)

Note: Nutritional values are approximate and can vary based on specific ingredient brands and quantities used.

Cooking Tips

- **Selecting Nuts:** Opt for raw or dry-roasted nuts without added salt to keep the sodium content low. If you prefer a bit of crunch, lightly toast the nuts in a dry skillet over medium heat for 3-5 minutes before mixing them with the dried fruits.
- **Choosing Dried Fruits:** Look for unsweetened and sulfite-free dried fruits to avoid added sugars and preservatives. Organic options are also a great choice for higher-quality ingredients.
- **Portion Control:** Nuts and dried fruits are calorie-dense, so it's important to be mindful of portion sizes. A small handful is usually sufficient to provide a satisfying and nutritious snack.
- **Customizing the Mix:** Feel free to customize the mix based on your taste preferences or nutritional goals. You can add seeds like pumpkin or sunflower seeds for extra crunch, or include dried coconut flakes for a tropical twist.
- **Storage:** Store the mixed nuts and dried fruits in an airtight container in a cool, dry place. This mix can last for several weeks if stored properly, making it a convenient option to have on hand.

Health Benefits

- **Rich in Healthy Fats:** Nuts are an excellent source of healthy fats, particularly monounsaturated and polyunsaturated fats, which are beneficial for heart health. These fats may help decrease bad cholesterol and minimize the risk of heart disease.

- **Good Source of Protein:** Nuts provide a plant-based source of protein, which is essential for building and repairing tissues, supporting immune function, and maintaining muscle mass.
- **High in Fiber:** Both nuts and dried fruits contribute to the fiber content of this snack. Fiber is important for digestive health, helping to regulate bowel movements and prevent constipation. It also plays a role in controlling blood sugar levels and maintaining a healthy weight.
- **Packed with Antioxidants:** Nuts, particularly walnuts and almonds, are rich in antioxidants like vitamin E, which help protect the body from oxidative stress and inflammation. Dried fruits like raisins and cranberries also contain antioxidants, including polyphenols, which support overall health.
- **Energy Boosting:** The combination of healthy fats, protein, and natural sugars from dried fruits provides a steady source of energy. This makes mixed nuts and dried fruits an ideal snack for staying energized throughout the day, especially during long work days or before workouts.
- **Supports Heart Health:** The healthy fats, fiber, and antioxidants found in nuts and dried fruits are beneficial for heart health. Regular consumption of these foods can help reduce the risk of cardiovascular disease by improving cholesterol levels and reducing inflammation.
- **Nutrient-Dense:** Nuts and dried fruits are packed with essential vitamins and minerals, including magnesium, potassium, and vitamin B6. These nutrients play a crucial role in various bodily functions, from maintaining healthy bones to supporting nerve function.
- **Kidney-Friendly Option:** When consumed in moderation and with careful selection of ingredients, this snack can fit into a kidney-friendly diet. For those managing kidney health, it's important to be mindful of portion sizes and to choose low-sodium and low-potassium options when possible.
- **Versatile and Convenient:** Mixed nuts and dried fruits are incredibly versatile and can be enjoyed in various ways. They can be eaten on their own, added to yogurt or salads, or used as a topping for oatmeal. Their long shelf life and portability make them a convenient snack option for busy lifestyles.

27. Yogurt Parfait with Honey

Preparation Time

- **10 minutes**

Cooking Time

- **None**

Serving Unit

- **2 servings**

Ingredients

- **1 cup plain Greek yogurt**
- **1/2 cup fresh berries (e.g., strawberries, blueberries, raspberries)**
- **1/4 cup granola (preferably low-sugar)**
- **2 tablespoons honey**
- **Optional toppings: sliced almonds, chia seeds, shredded coconut**

Procedures of Preparation

1. **Prepare the Ingredients:**
   - Wash and dry the fresh berries. If the strawberries are large, slice them into smaller pieces.
2. **Layer the Parfait:**
   - Take two serving glasses or bowls. Start by spooning half of the Greek yogurt into the bottom of each glass.
   - Add a layer of fresh berries over the yogurt, followed by a sprinkle of granola.
   - Repeat the layers, adding the remaining yogurt, more berries, and another layer of granola.
3. **Drizzle with Honey:**
   - Drizzle 1 tablespoon of honey over each parfait, allowing it to flow down through the layers.
4. **Add Optional Toppings:**

- If desired, top with sliced almonds, chia seeds, or shredded coconut for added texture and nutrients.

5. **Serve Immediately:**
    - Enjoy the parfait immediately while the granola is still crunchy.

Nutritional Values (Per Serving)

- **Calories:** 250-300 (varies based on specific types and quantities of ingredients used)
- **Protein:** 10-12g
- **Carbohydrates:** 40-45g
- **Fat:** 5-8g
- **Fiber:** 3-5g
- **Calcium:** 15-20% of the Daily Value
- **Sugar:** 20-25g (including natural sugars from fruit and honey)

Note: Nutritional values are approximate and can vary based on specific ingredient brands and quantities used.

Cooking Tips

- **Choose the Right Yogurt:** Greek yogurt is preferred for its thick and creamy texture, as well as its higher protein content. If you prefer a milder flavor, you can use plain yogurt, but keep in mind that it may be thinner.
- **Fresh vs. Frozen Berries:** Fresh berries are ideal for this recipe, but if they're out of season, you can use frozen berries. Just thaw them slightly before layering.
- **Granola Options:** Opt for a granola that is low in added sugars and made with whole grains. You can also make your own granola for a healthier option. If you want a lower-calorie parfait, you can reduce the amount of granola or replace it with nuts or seeds.
- **Honey Variations:** For a different flavor, try using flavored honey, such as lavender or orange blossom. If you're looking to cut down on sugar, you can reduce the amount of honey or use a sugar-free sweetener.
- **Make-Ahead Option:** If you're short on time in the morning, prepare the parfait the night before, but keep the granola separate to avoid it becoming soggy. Add the granola just before serving.

Health Benefits

- **High in Protein:** Greek yogurt is a high-protein food that promotes muscle repair and development. A high-protein breakfast can help keep you full and satisfied throughout the morning, reducing the temptation to snack on less healthy options.

- **Rich in Probiotics:** The live cultures in yogurt, known as probiotics, support gut health by promoting a healthy balance of bacteria in the digestive system. This may aid digestion, increase immunological function, and even improve mood.
- **Packed with Antioxidants:** Berries are rich in antioxidants, particularly vitamin C and flavonoids, which help protect the body against oxidative stress and inflammation. Antioxidants also support healthy skin and may reduce the risk of chronic diseases.
- **Bone Health Support:** Yogurt is a good source of calcium, which is crucial for maintaining strong bones and teeth. Regular consumption of calcium-rich foods like yogurt can help prevent osteoporosis and bone fractures.
- **Heart-Healthy Fats:** If you add nuts or seeds to your parfait, you'll benefit from heart-healthy fats, including omega-3 fatty acids. These fats can help reduce inflammation, lower bad cholesterol levels, and support overall cardiovascular health.
- **Energy-Boosting Carbohydrates:** The combination of honey, fruit, and granola provides a quick source of carbohydrates, which are essential for energy. This makes the parfait a great option before or after a workout.
- **Kidney-Friendly Option:** By choosing low-sodium and low-phosphorus options for the yogurt and granola, this parfait can fit into a kidney-friendly diet. The potassium content from the berries is also balanced by the protein in the yogurt, making it a suitable option for those managing kidney health.
- **Versatile and Customizable:** This parfait can be easily adapted to suit dietary preferences or restrictions. Whether you're looking to increase fiber, add more protein, or reduce sugar, the ingredients can be adjusted to meet your needs.

28. Edamame Beans with Sea Salt

Preparation Time

- **5 minutes**

Cooking Time

- **5-7 minutes**

Serving Unit

- **2 servings**

Ingredients

- **1 cup edamame beans (in the pod, fresh or frozen)**
- **1/2 teaspoon sea salt**
- **Optional: a pinch of chili flakes or a drizzle of sesame oil for extra flavor**

Procedures of Preparation

1. **Prepare the Edamame:**
    - If using fresh edamame, rinse them thoroughly under cold water. If using frozen edamame, no need to thaw; simply remove them from the freezer.
2. **Boil the Edamame:**
    - Bring a pot of water to a boil. Add the edamame beans to the boiling water and cook for 5-7 minutes, or until the beans are tender. They should be bright green and easily pop out of their pods.
3. **Drain and Season:**
    - Drain the edamame beans in a colander and allow them to cool slightly.
    - While still warm, sprinkle the edamame with sea salt. If desired, you can also add a pinch of chili flakes for a bit of heat or a drizzle of sesame oil for added richness.
4. **Serve:**

- Transfer the seasoned edamame to a serving bowl. To eat, simply pop the beans out of the pods and enjoy.

Nutritional Values (Per Serving)

- **Calories:** 120-140 (depending on the amount of seasoning used)
- **Protein:** 10-12g
- **Carbohydrates:** 10-12g
- **Fat:** 4-5g
- **Fiber:** 4-5g
- **Sodium:** 300-400mg (varies based on the amount of salt added)
- **Iron:** 10% of the Daily Value

Note: Nutritional values are approximate and can vary based on specific ingredient brands and quantities used.

Cooking Tips

- **Selecting Edamame:** Fresh edamame can usually be found in the produce section of grocery stores, while frozen edamame is typically located in the freezer aisle. Both fresh and frozen edamame work well for this recipe.
- **Boiling Time:** Be careful not to overcook the edamame, as this can cause them to become mushy. The beans should be tender but still firm to the bite.
- **Serving Suggestions:** Edamame can be enjoyed on its own as a snack, or it can be added to salads, stir-fries, or grain bowls for extra protein and texture.
- **Spicing It Up:** For a more flavorful twist, try adding other seasonings like garlic powder, smoked paprika, or nutritional yeast. These can enhance the taste without adding too many extra calories.
- **Storage:** Cooked edamame can be stored in an airtight container in the refrigerator for up to 3 days. Reheat gently in the microwave before serving, or enjoy them cold as a snack.

Health Benefits

- **High in Plant-Based Protein:** Edamame is an excellent source of plant-based protein, making it a great snack option for vegetarians, vegans, and anyone looking to increase their protein intake. Protein is necessary for muscle repair, immunological function, and general cell health.
- **Rich in Fiber:** The high fiber content in edamame aids in digestion, helps regulate blood sugar levels, and promotes a feeling of fullness, which can support weight management.
- **Heart-Healthy Fats:** Edamame contains heart-healthy

unsaturated fats, which can help lower bad cholesterol levels and reduce the risk of heart disease.

- **Supports Bone Health:** Edamame is a good source of calcium, magnesium, and vitamin K, all of which are important for maintaining strong bones and preventing osteoporosis.
- **Rich in Antioxidants:** Edamame is packed with antioxidants, including isoflavones, which have been shown to reduce inflammation and may help lower the risk of certain chronic diseases, including heart disease and certain cancers.
- **Kidney-Friendly Option:** Edamame can be a suitable option for those managing kidney health, as it is low in phosphorus and provides high-quality protein. However, it's important to moderate the amount of sodium by controlling the sea salt added.
- **Supports Healthy Weight:** The combination of protein and fiber in edamame helps to control appetite and promote satiety, making it a smart choice for those looking to maintain or lose weight.
- **Versatile Snack:** Edamame is a versatile snack that can be enjoyed in various ways. Whether you prefer them lightly salted, spiced up with chili flakes, or drizzled with sesame oil, edamame offers a tasty and nutritious snack that can be easily customized to suit your preferences.

5

Desserts

29. Baked Apples with Cinnamon

Preparation Time

- 15 minutes

Cooking Time

- 25-30 minutes

Serving Unit

- 4 servings

Ingredients

- 4 medium apples (e.g., Honeycrisp, Granny Smith)
- 2 tablespoons brown sugar (or a sugar substitute)
- 1 teaspoon ground cinnamon
- 1/4 teaspoon ground nutmeg
- 1/4 cup chopped nuts (e.g., walnuts, pecans)
- 2 tablespoons raisins or dried cranberries (optional)
- 1 tablespoon melted butter or coconut oil
- 1/4 cup water
- Vanilla yogurt or ice cream for serving (optional)

Procedures of Preparation

1. **Preheat the Oven:**
   - Preheat your oven to 350°F (175°C).
2. **Prepare the Apples:**
   - Wash and core the apples, removing the seeds and creating a hollow space in the center. You can use an apple corer or a small knife to do this.
3. **Mix the Filling:**
   - In a small bowl, combine the brown sugar, ground cinnamon, ground nutmeg, and chopped nuts. If using raisins or dried cranberries, mix them in as well.
4. **Stuff the Apples:**
   - Spoon the sugar and spice mixture into the

hollowed-out centers of the apples. Press down gently to pack the filling.

5. **Prepare for Baking:**
   - Place the stuffed apples in a baking dish. Drizzle the melted butter or coconut oil over the apples. Add 1/4 cup of water to the baking dish to help create steam and keep the apples moist during baking.
6. **Bake the Apples:**
   - Bake in a preheated oven for 25-30 minutes, or until the apples are soft when pricked with a fork. The baking time may vary depending on the size and type of apples used.
7. **Serve:**
   - Take the apples out of the oven and allow them to cool slightly before serving. For an extra treat, top with a dollop of vanilla yogurt or a scoop of ice cream if desired.

Nutritional Values (Per Serving)

- **Calories:** 150-200 (varies based on sugar and topping used)
- **Protein:** 2-3g
- **Carbohydrates:** 35-40g
- **Fat:** 6-8g (depending on butter or oil used)
- **Fiber:** 4-5g
- **Sugar:** 20-25g (including natural sugars from apples and added sugar)

Note: Nutritional values are approximate and can vary based on specific ingredient brands and quantities used.

Cooking Tips

- **Apple Varieties:** Choose firm apples that hold up well during baking, such as Honeycrisp or Granny Smith. Softer apples like Red Delicious may become mushy.
- **Adjust Sweetness:** Feel free to adjust the amount of brown sugar or use a sugar substitute if you're looking to reduce sugar intake.
- **Add Flavor:** Experiment with additional spices like cloves or ginger to customize the flavor of the filling.
- **Keep Apples Moist:** Adding a small amount of water to the baking dish helps prevent the apples from drying out and creates a delicious sauce in the bottom of the dish.
- **Serve Warm:** Baked apples are best enjoyed warm. If preparing in advance, reheat in the microwave or oven before serving.

Health Benefits

- **Rich in Fiber:** Apples are a good source of dietary fiber, which aids in digestion and helps maintain healthy bowel movements.
- **Low in Calories:** Baked apples are a lower-calorie dessert option compared to many traditional sweets, making them a good choice for weight management.
- **Antioxidants:** Apples are rich in antioxidants like vitamin C and flavonoids, which help protect the body from oxidative stress and support overall health.
- **Heart Health:** The fiber in apples can help lower cholesterol levels and support cardiovascular health.
- **Blood Sugar Control:** The natural sugars in apples are balanced with fiber, which helps regulate blood sugar levels and provides a steady source of energy.
- **Bone Health:** Apples contain small amounts of calcium and potassium, which support bone health and muscle function.
- **Kidney-Friendly:** This recipe is suitable for kidney-friendly diets when prepared with minimal added sugar and low-sodium ingredients.

30. Fresh Fruit Salad with Mint

Preparation Time

- **15 minutes**

Cooking Time

- **None**

Serving Unit

- **4 servings**

Ingredients

- **1 cup strawberries, hulled and sliced**
- **1 cup blueberries**
- **1 cup grapes, halved**
- **1 cup diced mango**
- **1 cup diced kiwi**
- **1 tablespoon fresh mint leaves, finely chopped**
- **1 tablespoon honey or agave syrup (optional)**
- **Juice of 1 lime**

Procedures of Preparation

1. **Prepare the Fruit:**
   - Wash and prepare all the fruit. Hull and slice the strawberries, halve the grapes, and dice the mango and kiwi into bite-sized pieces.
2. **Combine the Fruit:**
   - In a large mixing bowl, gently combine the strawberries, blueberries, grapes, mango, and kiwi.
3. **Add Mint and Sweetener:**
   - Sprinkle the chopped mint leaves over the fruit. If desired, drizzle with honey or agave syrup for added sweetness.
4. **Add Lime Juice:**
   - Squeeze the juice of one lime over the fruit salad. This not only adds a tangy flavor but also helps to

preserve the freshness of the fruit.

5. **Toss and Serve:**
   - Gently mix the fruit salad to blend the ingredients. Serve right away or refrigerated until ready to use.

Nutritional Values (Per Serving)

- **Calories:** 100-150 (depending on the fruit and optional sweetener used)
- **Protein:** 1-2g
- **Carbohydrates:** 25-30g
- **Fat:** 0.5g
- **Fiber:** 4-5g
- **Sugar:** 15-20g (natural sugars from fruit)

Note: Nutritional values are approximate and can vary based on specific fruit types and quantities used.

Cooking Tips

- **Fruit Selection:** Use a variety of fruits to add different textures and flavors to your salad. Choose fruits that are in season for the best flavor and freshness.
- **Chop Evenly:** Cut the fruit into uniform pieces to ensure even distribution and a pleasing presentation.
- **Additions:** Consider adding a handful of nuts or seeds for extra crunch and nutrition. You can also mix in a small amount of shredded coconut for added flavor.
- **Mint Preparation:** For a more intense mint flavor, bruise the mint leaves slightly before chopping. This releases more of the mint's essential oils.
- **Refrigeration:** The fruit salad can be prepared a few hours in advance. Keep it covered in the refrigerator until serving to maintain its freshness.

Health Benefits

- **High in Vitamins:** This fruit salad is rich in vitamins A, C, and K, which support immune function, skin health, and bone health.
- **Rich in Antioxidants:** Fruits like blueberries and strawberries are high in antioxidants, which help protect the body from oxidative stress and support overall health.
- **Hydration:** Fruits have high water content, which helps keep the body hydrated and supports overall well-being.
- **Fiber-Rich:** The fiber from fruits aids in digestion, helps regulate blood sugar levels, and promotes a feeling of fullness, which can assist with weight management.
- **Low in Calories:** Fresh fruit salad is a low-calorie,

nutrient-dense option that can be enjoyed as part of a balanced diet.

- **Kidney-Friendly:** The fruit salad can be adapted to meet kidney-friendly dietary needs by choosing fruits that are lower in potassium and avoiding added sugars.
- **Digestive Health:** The combination of fruit and mint aids in digestion and can help soothe the digestive tract.

31. Berry Sorbet

Preparation Time

- **15 minutes**

Cooking Time

- **None** (Chilling time required)

Serving Unit

- **4 servings**

Ingredients

- **2 cups mixed berries (strawberries, raspberries, blueberries, or blackberries)**
- **1/2 cup water**
- **1/2 cup honey or agave syrup (or to taste)**
- **1 tablespoon lemon juice**
- **1/2 teaspoon vanilla extract (optional)**

Procedures of Preparation

1. **Prepare the Berries:**
    - Wash the berries thoroughly. If using strawberries, hull and slice them. For other berries, simply rinse and pat dry.
2. **Blend the Mixture:**
    - In a food processor or blender, mix the berries, water, honey or agave syrup, and lemon juice. Blend until smooth.
3. **Strain (Optional):**
    - For a smoother texture, strain the mixture through a fine mesh sieve to remove seeds and any pulp. This step is optional but recommended for a silkier sorbet.
4. **Freeze the Mixture:**
    - Pour the berry mixture into a shallow, freezer-safe dish. Place it in the freezer and stir every 30 minutes with a fork to break up any

ice crystals, for about 2-3 hours, until the sorbet is firm and scoopable.

5. **Serve:**
    - When the sorbet is completely frozen, scoop it into dishes and serve immediately. Garnish with fresh mint or additional berries if desired.

Nutritional Values (Per Serving)

- **Calories:** 80-100
- **Protein:** 1g
- **Carbohydrates:** 20g
- **Fat:** 0g
- **Fiber:** 3g
- **Sugar:** 15g (includes natural sugars from berries and added sweetener)

Note: Nutritional values are approximate and can differ based on specific ingredients and quantities used.

Cooking Tips

- **Use Fresh or Frozen Berries:** Both fresh and frozen berries work well for this recipe. If using frozen berries, let them defrost somewhat before mixing.
- **Adjust Sweetness:** Taste the mixture before freezing and adjust the sweetness as needed. Depending on the ripeness of your berries, you may need more or less sweetener.
- **Break Up Ice Crystals:** To ensure a smooth texture, stir the mixture every 30 minutes while freezing. This prevents large ice crystals from forming and keeps the sorbet creamy.
- **Serve Quickly:** Berry sorbet is best enjoyed right after it's frozen to maintain its optimal texture. If it becomes too hard, let it sit at room temperature for a few minutes to soften slightly before serving.

Health Benefits

- **Rich in Antioxidants:** Berries are high in antioxidants, including vitamin C and flavonoids, which help protect the body from oxidative stress and support immune function.
- **Low in Calories:** Berry sorbet is a low-calorie dessert option compared to many traditional sweets, making it a good choice for weight management.
- **Hydrating:** The high water content in berries contributes to hydration and supports overall health.
- **Fiber-Rich:** Berries provide dietary fiber, which aids in digestion and helps maintain healthy bowel movements.
- **Natural Sweetener:** Using honey or agave syrup as a sweetener offers a more natural

alternative to refined sugars, reducing the overall glycemic impact of the dessert.

32. Greek Yogurt Cheesecake

Preparation Time

- 20 minutes

Cooking Time

- 45-50 minutes

Cooling Time

- 4 hours (minimum)

Serving Unit

- 8 servings

Ingredients

Crust:

- **1 cup graham cracker crumbs**
- **2 tablespoons coconut oil or melted butter**
- **2 tablespoons honey or maple syrup**

Filling:

- **8 oz (225g) reduced-fat cream cheese, softened**
- **2 cups plain Greek yogurt (non-fat or low-fat)**
- **1/2 cup honey or maple syrup**
- **3 large eggs**
- **1 teaspoon vanilla extract**
- **1 tablespoon all-purpose flour (optional, for added thickness)**

Procedures of Preparation

1. **Preheat the Oven:**
   - Preheat your oven to 325°F (165°C).
2. **Prepare the Crust:**
   - In a medium mixing bowl, combine graham cracker crumbs, melted coconut oil or butter, and honey or maple syrup until thoroughly blended.
   - Press the mixture into the bottom of a 9-inch springform pan to create

an equal layer. Using the back of a spoon, push it firmly.

3. **Prepare the Filling:**
    - In a large mixing bowl, whip the softened cream cheese until smooth and creamy.
    - Add the Greek yogurt and honey or maple syrup, and mix until well combined.
    - Beat in the eggs one at a time, making sure each egg is completely mixed before adding the next.
    - Stir in the vanilla extract and flour if using.
4. **Assemble the Cheesecake:**
    - Pour the filling over the prepared crust in the springform pan. Smooth the top with a spatula.
5. **Bake the Cheesecake:**
    -
    -
    - Bake in a preheated oven for 45-50 minutes, or until the center is firm and the sides are lightly golden
    - . The center may still be slightly jiggly but will firm up as it cools.
6. **Cool and Chill:**
    - Allow the cheesecake to cool in the pan on a wire rack for about 1 hour. Once cooled, cover and refrigerate for at least 4 hours or overnight for best results.
7. **Serve:**
    - Run a knife around the edge of the pan to loosen the cheesecake before removing the sides of the springform pan. Slice and serve chilled. Garnish with fresh fruit or a drizzle of honey if desired.

Nutritional Values (Per Serving)

- **Calories:** 200-250
- **Protein:** 10-12g
- **Carbohydrates:** 22-25g
- **Fat:** 8-10g
- **Fiber:** 1g
- **Sugar:** 15-18g (includes natural sugars from Greek yogurt and added sweetener)

Note: Nutritional values are approximate and can differ based on specific ingredients and quantities used.

Cooking Tips

- **Use Room Temperature Ingredients:** Ensure that the cream cheese and Greek yogurt are at room temperature to avoid lumps and ensure a smooth filling.
- **Check for Doneness:** The cheesecake is finished when the borders are firm and the middle is slightly jiggly. Overbaking may lead to cracks and a dry texture.

- **Prevent Cracks:** Bake the cheesecake in a water bath to avoid cracks. Place the springform pan in a larger baking dish filled with hot water while baking. This helps maintain a consistent temperature and prevents cracking.
- **Chill Thoroughly:** Allow the cheesecake to cool completely before refrigerating. Chilling it overnight helps the flavors meld and improves the texture.
- **Garnish Options:** Top the cheesecake with fresh fruit, a berry compote, or a sprinkle of nuts for added flavor and texture.

Health Benefits

- **High in Protein:** Greek yogurt is rich in protein, which supports muscle health and keeps you feeling full and satisfied.
- **Lower in Fat:** Using reduced-fat cream cheese and Greek yogurt reduces the overall fat content compared to traditional cheesecake recipes.
- **Calcium-Rich:** Greek yogurt and cream cheese provide calcium, which is essential for maintaining strong bones and teeth.
- **Probiotics:** Greek yogurt contains probiotics, which support gut health and boost the immune system.
- **Lower Sugar:** By using natural sweeteners like honey or maple syrup, you can reduce the amount of refined sugar in the dessert.
- **Kidney-Friendly:** This cheesecake can be adapted for kidney-friendly diets by using lower-fat cream cheese and controlling added sugars.

33. Coconut Rice Pudding

Preparation Time

- 10 minutes

Cooking Time

- 35-40 minutes

Serving Unit

- 4 servings

Ingredients

- **1 cup jasmine rice**
- **1 can (13.5 oz) full-fat coconut milk**
- **2 cups water**
- **1/2 cup maple syrup or honey**
- **1/4 cup shredded coconut (unsweetened)**
- **1/2 teaspoon vanilla extract**
- **1/4 teaspoon ground cinnamon**
- **Pinch of salt**

Procedures of Preparation

1. **Rinse the Rice:**
   - Rinse the jasmine rice in cool water until it is clear. This helps to eliminate extra starch and keep the pudding from getting too thick.
2. **Cook the Rice:**
   - In a medium saucepan, mix together the washed rice, coconut milk, and water. Bring to a boil over a medium to high heat.
3. **Simmer the Mixture:**
   - Reduce the heat to low, cover, and simmer for 20-25 minutes, or until the rice is tender and the liquid is mostly absorbed. Stir occasionally to prevent sticking.
4. **Add Sweeteners and Flavors:**

- Stir in the maple syrup or honey, shredded coconut, vanilla extract, ground cinnamon, and a pinch of salt. Continue to cook for an additional 10-15 minutes, or until the pudding reaches a creamy consistency and has thickened to your liking.

5. **Serve:**
    - Take out the saucepan from the heat and allow the pudding to cool slightly. Serve warm or chilled. Garnish with additional shredded coconut or fresh fruit if desired.

Nutritional Values (Per Serving)

- **Calories:** 250-300
- **Protein:** 3g
- **Carbohydrates:** 45g
- **Fat:** 10g
- **Fiber:** 2g
- **Sugar:** 20g (includes natural sugars from coconut milk and added sweetener)

Note: Nutritional values are approximate and can differ based on specific ingredients and quantities used.

Cooking Tips

- **Use Full-Fat Coconut Milk:** For a richer, creamier pudding, use full-fat coconut milk. Light coconut milk can be used for a lower fat version but will result in a less creamy texture.
- **Stir Frequently:** Stir the pudding regularly during cooking to prevent the rice from sticking to the bottom of the pan and to ensure even cooking.
- **Adjust Sweetness:** Taste the pudding before removing it from the heat and adjust the sweetness according to your preference. You can add more maple syrup or honey if desired.
- **Cool and Thicken:** The pudding will thicken further as it cools. If it becomes too thick after cooling, stir in a little extra coconut milk to reach your desired consistency.
- **Garnish Ideas:** Top with fresh fruit, a sprinkle of cinnamon, or a dollop of coconut whipped cream for extra flavor and texture.

Health Benefits

- **Dairy-Free:** Coconut milk is a great alternative for those who are lactose intolerant or following a dairy-free diet.
- **Rich in Healthy Fats:** The fats from coconut milk can provide sustained energy and support heart health.
- **Natural Sweeteners:** Using maple syrup or honey instead of

refined sugars can reduce the overall glycemic load of the dessert.

- **Gluten-Free:** This recipe is naturally gluten-free, making it suitable for those with celiac disease or gluten sensitivity.
- **Fiber-Rich:** The addition of shredded coconut adds dietary fiber, which aids in digestion and helps maintain a healthy digestive system.

34. Peach and Berry Crisp

Preparation Time

- 15 minutes

Cooking Time

- 35-40 minutes

Serving Unit

- 6 servings

Ingredients

Filling:

- **4 cups fresh peaches, peeled and sliced (about 4 large peaches)**
- **2 cups mixed berries (blueberries, raspberries, and blackberries)**
- **1/4 cup honey or maple syrup**
- **1 tablespoon lemon juice**
- **1 tablespoon cornstarch**
- **1/2 teaspoon ground cinnamon**

Topping:

- **1 cup rolled oats**
- **1/2 cup almond flour**
- **1/4 cup coconut oil or butter, melted**
- **1/4 cup honey or maple syrup**
- **1/4 cup chopped nuts (e.g., almonds or walnuts)**
- **1/4 teaspoon ground cinnamon**

Procedures of Preparation

1. **Preheat the Oven:**
   - Preheat your oven to 350°F (175°C).
2. **Prepare the Filling:**
   - In a large bowl, combine the sliced peaches and mixed berries. Add the honey or maple syrup,

lemon juice, cornstarch, and ground cinnamon. Toss until the fruit is properly coated..

3. **Assemble the Filling:**
    - Transfer the fruit mixture to a 9x13-inch baking dish and spread it out evenly.
4. **Prepare the Topping:**
    - In a separate bowl, mix together the rolled oats, almond flour, melted coconut oil or butter, honey or maple syrup, chopped nuts, and ground cinnamon until well combined.
5. **Add the Topping:**
    - Sprinkle the oat mixture evenly over the fruit filling in the baking dish.
6. **Bake:**
    - Bake in the preheated oven for 35-40 minutes, or until the topping is golden brown and the fruit is bubbling. You can test the crisp by inserting a fork into the fruit; it should be tender.
7. **Serve:**
    - Let the crisp cool slightly before serving. Enjoy warm or at room temperature, with a scoop of vanilla yogurt or a dollop of whipped cream if desired.

Nutritional Values (Per Serving)

- **Calories:** 220-270
- **Protein:** 3g
- **Carbohydrates:** 35g
- **Fat:** 10g
- **Fiber:** 4g
- **Sugar:** 20g (includes natural sugars from fruit and added sweetener)

Note: Nutritional values are approximate and can differ based on specific ingredients and quantities used.

Cooking Tips

- **Use Fresh or Frozen Fruit:** You can use fresh or frozen peaches and berries. If using frozen fruit, do not thaw it before baking; just add a few extra minutes to the baking time.
- **Adjust Sweetness:** Depending on the sweetness of your fruit, you may need to adjust the amount of honey or maple syrup. Taste the filling before baking and adjust as needed.
- **Make Ahead:** This crisp can be prepared ahead of time and stored in the refrigerator. Reheat in the oven before serving for a warm dessert.
- **Check for Doneness:** Ensure the topping is golden brown and the fruit is bubbling before removing the crisp from the oven. This indicates that the filling is

fully cooked and the topping is crisp.

- **Serve with Toppings:** Enhance the crisp by serving it with a scoop of vanilla ice cream, a dollop of Greek yogurt, or a drizzle of cream.

Health Benefits

- **Rich in Vitamins:** Peaches and berries are rich in vitamins A and C, which support immune function and skin health.
- **Antioxidants:** Berries are high in antioxidants, which help protect against oxidative stress and inflammation.
- **Whole Grains:** The rolled oats in the topping provide dietary fiber and essential nutrients, including iron and magnesium.
- **Natural Sweeteners:** Using honey or maple syrup as a sweetener reduces the glycemic impact compared to refined sugars.
- **Nutrient-Dense:** The addition of nuts and almond flour adds healthy fats and protein, contributing to overall satiety and balanced nutrition.

35. Almond Flour Cookies

Preparation Time

- 15 minutes

Cooking Time

- 10-12 minutes

Serving Unit

- 12 cookies

Ingredients

- **2 cups almond flour**
- **1/2 cup coconut sugar or granulated erythritol**
- **1/4 cup coconut oil or unsalted butter, melted**
- **1 large egg**
- **1 teaspoon vanilla extract**
- **1/2 teaspoon baking soda**
- **1/4 teaspoon salt**
- **1/4 cup chopped almonds or dark chocolate chips (optional)**

Procedures of Preparation

1. **Preheat the Oven:**
   - Preheat the oven to 350°F/175°C and line a baking sheet using parchment paper.
2. **Mix the Dry Ingredients:**
   - In a large bowl, whisk together the almond flour, coconut sugar (or erythritol), baking soda, and salt until well combined.
3. **Combine Wet Ingredients:**
   - In a separate bowl, mix together the melted coconut oil (or butter), egg, and vanilla extract until smooth and well blended.
4. **Combine Wet and Dry Ingredients:**
   - Add the wet components to the dry ones and mix

until a dough forms. If using, fold in the chopped almonds or dark chocolate chips.

5. **Shape the Cookies:**
   - Use a tablespoon or cookie scoop to drop spoonfuls of dough onto the prepared baking sheet. Flatten each cookie gently with the back of a spoon for even baking.
6. **Bake:**
   - Bake for 10-12 minutes in a preheated oven, or until golden brown around the edges. The cores should be firm but somewhat soft.
7. **Cool:**
   - Leave the cookies on the baking sheet to cool for 5 minutes before moving them to a wire rack to finish cooling.
8. **Serve:**
   - Enjoy the cookies as a sweet treat on their own or with a glass of almond milk or tea.

Nutritional Values (Per Cookie)

- **Calories:** 120
- **Protein:** 3g
- **Carbohydrates:** 8g
- **Fat:** 9g
- **Fiber:** 2g
- **Sugar:** 4g (includes natural sugars from coconut sugar or erythritol)

Note: Nutritional values are approximate and can differ based on specific ingredients and quantities used.

Cooking Tips

- **Chill the Dough:** For a firmer dough that's easier to handle, chill it in the refrigerator for 15-30 minutes before baking.
- **Watch the Baking Time:** Almond flour cookies can brown quickly, so keep an eye on them towards the end of the baking time to avoid burning.
- **Use Parchment Paper:** Line your baking sheet with parchment paper to prevent sticking and to make cleanup easier.
- **Customize Flavors:** Add spices like cinnamon or nutmeg for extra flavor, or mix in dried fruit, coconut flakes, or a touch of sea salt for variety.
- **Storage:** Store cookies in an airtight container at room temperature for up to a week, or freeze for longer storage.

Health Benefits

- **Gluten-Free:** Almond flour is naturally gluten-free, making these cookies suitable for those with celiac disease or gluten intolerance.

- **Rich in Healthy Fats:** Almond flour is a good source of healthy monounsaturated fats, which support heart health and provide sustained energy.
- **High in Protein:** Almonds are high in protein compared to other flours, which helps with muscle repair and growth.
- **Low-Carb:** Almond flour is lower in carbohydrates than wheat flour, making these cookies a good option for those on low-carb or ketogenic diets.
- **Nutrient-Dense:** Almonds provide important nutrients like vitamin E, magnesium, and calcium, which contribute to overall health and well-being.

6
Flavorful Soups and Stews

36. Hearty Chicken and Vegetable Stew

Preparation Time

- 20 minutes

Cooking Time

- 1 hour

Serving Unit

- 6 servings

Ingredients

- 1 pound (450 grams) boneless, skinless chicken thighs or breasts, chopped into bite-sized pieces
- 2 tablespoons olive oil
- 1 large onion, diced
- 3 cloves garlic, minced
- 3 carrots, sliced
- 2 celery stalks, chopped
- 1 cup green beans, trimmed and chopped into one-inch pieces
- 2 cups potatoes, peeled and cubed
- 1 cup frozen peas
-
-
- 1 (14.5 oz) can of diced tomatoes with no salt added
-
- 4 cups low-sodium chicken broth
- 1 teaspoon dried thyme
- 1 teaspoon dried rosemary
- 1 bay leaf
- Salt and pepper, to taste
- 2 tablespoons fresh parsley, chopped (for garnish)

Procedures of Preparation

1. **Heat the Oil:**
    - Heat the olive oil in a big saucepan or Dutch oven over medium heat.
2. **Cook the Chicken:**
    - Add the diced chicken to the pot and cook until

browned on all sides, about 5-7 minutes. Take the chicken out of the pot and leave aside.

3. **Sauté Vegetables:**
   - In the same pot, add the onion and garlic. Sauté the onion for approximately 3-4 minutes, or until transparent and aromatic.
4. **Add Carrots and Celery:**
   - Stir in the carrots and celery and cook for another 5 minutes.
5. **Combine Ingredients:**
   - Return the browned chicken to the pot. Add the potatoes, green beans, peas, diced tomatoes, and chicken broth. Stir to combine.
6. **Season and Simmer:**
   - Mix in the dried thyme, rosemary, bay leaf, salt, and pepper. Bring the mixture to a boil.
7. **Cook the Stew:**
   - Reduce the heat to low, cover, and simmer for 40-50 minutes, or until the vegetables are tender and the chicken is cooked through.
8. **Finish and Serve:**
   - Remove the bay leaf. Taste and adjust seasoning if necessary. Garnish with fresh parsley before serving.

Nutritional Values (Per Serving)

- **Calories:** 250
- **Protein:** 20g
- **Carbohydrates:** 30g
- **Fat:** 8g
- **Fiber:** 5g
- **Sugar:** 6g

Note: Nutritional values are approximate and can differ based on specific ingredients and quantities used.

Cooking Tips

- **Brown the Chicken Well:** Browning the chicken pieces before adding the vegetables enhances the flavor of the stew.
- **Use Fresh Herbs:** If possible, use fresh thyme and rosemary instead of dried for a more robust flavor.
- **Cut Vegetables Evenly:** To ensure even cooking, cut the vegetables into uniform pieces.
- **Adjust Thickness:** If you prefer a thicker stew, you can mash a portion of the potatoes with a fork or add a slurry of cornstarch and water.
- **Leftovers:** This stew keeps well in the refrigerator for up to 3 days and can be frozen for up to 3 months.

Health Benefits

- **Rich in Protein:** Chicken provides a lean source of protein essential for muscle repair and overall health.
- **Nutrient-Dense:** The variety of vegetables adds vitamins, minerals, and dietary fiber to the stew, promoting digestive health and overall well-being.
- **Low in Sodium:** Using low-sodium chicken broth helps keep the sodium content in check, making it a heart-healthy choice.
- **Comforting and Filling:** This stew is both satisfying and nourishing, providing a balanced meal that keeps you full and energized.

37. Low-Sodium Tomato Basil Soup

Preparation Time

- **15 minutes**

Cooking Time

- **25 minutes**

Serving Unit

- **4 servings**

Ingredients

- **2 tablespoons olive oil**
- **1 large onion, diced**
- **3 cloves garlic, minced**
- **1 (28 oz) can no-salt-added crushed tomatoes**
- **2 cups low-sodium vegetable broth**
- **1 teaspoon dried basil (or 2 tablespoons fresh basil minced)**
- **1/2 teaspoon dried oregano**
- **1/4 teaspoon black pepper**
- **1/4 teaspoon sugar (optional, to balance acidity)**
- **2 tablespoons fresh basil, chopped (for garnish)**
- **1 tablespoon lemon juice (optional, for brightness)**

Procedures of Preparation

1. **Heat the Oil:**
   - In a big pot, hot the olive oil over medium heat.
2. **Sauté Onion and Garlic:**
   - Add the chopped onion and garlic to the saucepan. Sauté for about 5 minutes, or until the onion is tender and transparent.
3. **Add Tomatoes and Broth:**
   - Stir in the crushed tomatoes and vegetable broth. Bring the mixture to a boil.
4. **Season the Soup:**

- Add the dried basil, oregano, black pepper, and sugar (if using). Stir well.

5. **Simmer:**
   - Reduce the heat to low and let the soup simmer for 15-20 minutes to allow the flavors to meld together.
6. **Blend the Soup:**
   - With an immersion blender, puree the soup until it is completely smooth. Alternatively, gently transfer the soup to a blender in batches.
7. **Adjust Seasoning:**
   - Taste the soup and adjust seasoning if needed. Stir in fresh basil and lemon juice (if using) just before serving.
8. **Serve:**
   - Ladle the soup into dishes and top with more fresh basil.

Nutritional Values (Per Serving)

- **Calories:** 130
- **Protein:** 3g
- **Carbohydrates:** 22g
- **Fat:** 6g
- **Fiber:** 4g
- **Sugar:** 12g

Note: Nutritional values are approximate and can differ based on specific ingredients and quantities used.

Cooking Tips

- **Use Fresh Herbs:** Fresh basil adds a bright, aromatic flavor. If using dried basil, be sure to use a bit less, as dried herbs are more concentrated.
- **Balance Acidity:** If the soup is too acidic, a small amount of sugar can help balance the flavors. Adjust to taste.
- **Blending Options:** For a chunkier soup, blend only half of the soup and leave the rest as-is. For a smooth texture, blend all of it.
- **Storage:** The soup can be stored in the refrigerator for up to 4 days or frozen for up to 3 months. Reheat gently before serving.

Health Benefits

- **Low in Sodium:** Using no-salt-added tomatoes and low-sodium broth keeps the sodium content low, which is beneficial for heart health.
- **Rich in Vitamins:** Tomatoes are rich in vitamins A and C, which support immune function and skin health.
- **Antioxidants:** Tomatoes contain lycopene, an antioxidant that has been linked to various health benefits, including reduced risk of certain cancers.
- **Fiber-Rich:** The soup provides dietary fiber from the tomatoes and vegetables, which aids in

digestion and helps maintain a healthy gut.

- **Hydrating:** With a high water content, this soup helps keep you hydrated and can be a good option for those needing to increase fluid intake.

38. Kidney-Friendly Minestrone Soup

Preparation Time

- 20 minutes

Cooking Time

- 40 minutes

Serving Unit

- 6 servings

Ingredients

- 2 tablespoons olive oil
- 1 large onion, diced
- 3 cloves garlic, minced
- 2 medium carrots, diced
- 2 celery stalks, diced
- 1 cup green beans, cut into 1-inch pieces
- 1 medium zucchini, diced
- 1 cup low-sodium vegetable broth
- 1 cup no-salt-added diced tomatoes
- 1/2 cup cooked pasta (such as ditalini or elbow macaroni)
- 1/2 cup kidney beans (canned, drained, and rinsed)
- 1 teaspoon dried basil
- 1 teaspoon dried oregano
- 1/2 teaspoon black pepper
- 1 bay leaf
- 1 cup baby spinach or kale (optional)
- 1 tablespoon fresh parsley, chopped (for garnish)

Procedures of Preparation

1. **Heat the Oil:**
   - In a large pot, heat the olive oil over medium heat.
2. **Sauté Vegetables:**
   - Sauté the onion and garlic until the onion is transparent, about 5 minutes. Add the carrots

and celery and cook for an additional 5 minutes.

3. **Add Remaining Vegetables:**
   - Stir in the green beans and zucchini, cooking for another 5 minutes.
4. **Add Broth and Tomatoes:**
   - Pour in the vegetable broth and diced tomatoes. Bring the mixture to a boil.
5. **Season the Soup:**
   - Add the dried basil, oregano, black pepper, and bay leaf. Stir well.
6. **Simmer:**
   - Reduce the heat to low and let the soup cook for 20 minutes, or until the vegetables are tender.
7. **Add Beans and Pasta:**
   - Stir in the cooked pasta and kidney beans. Continue to cook for another 5 minutes.
8. **Add Greens:**
   - If using, stir in the baby spinach or kale just before serving and cook until wilted.
9. **Garnish and Serve:**
   - Remove the bay leaf, and garnish with fresh parsley. Serve hot.

Nutritional Values (Per Serving)

- **Calories:** 150
- **Protein:** 7g
- **Carbohydrates:** 25g
- **Fat:** 4g
- **Fiber:** 6g
- **Sugar:** 6g
- **Potassium:** 400mg

Note: Nutritional values are approximate and can differ based on specific ingredients and quantities used.

Cooking Tips

- **Low-Sodium Broth:** Use a low-sodium or homemade vegetable broth to keep the sodium content in check.
- **Adjust Potassium:** For further potassium control, consider using less zucchini or replacing some ingredients with lower-potassium alternatives.
- **Flavor Boost:** If desired, add a splash of lemon juice or a dash of vinegar to enhance the soup's flavor.
- **Freeze for Later:** This soup freezes well. Let it cool completely before transferring to airtight containers for up to 3 months.

Health Benefits

- **Kidney-Friendly:** This soup is designed to be low in sodium and potassium, making it suitable for those managing kidney health.
- **Nutrient-Dense:** The variety of vegetables provides essential

vitamins, minerals, and dietary fiber.

- **Hydrating:** High water content helps with hydration and maintaining kidney function.
- **Heart-Healthy:** Olive oil provides healthy fats that support cardiovascular health.
- **Customizable:** You can adjust the recipe to include vegetables of your choice while keeping it within kidney-friendly guidelines.

39. Beef and Barley Soup with Fresh Herbs

Preparation Time

- **20 minutes**

Cooking Time

- **1 hour 15 minutes**

Serving Unit

- **6 servings**

Ingredients

- **2 tablespoons olive oil**
- **1 pound (450 grams) of beef stew meat (cut into bite-sized pieces)**
- **1 large onion, diced**
- **3 cloves garlic, minced**
- **2 carrots, sliced**
- **2 celery stalks, chopped**
- **1 cup barley (pearl or hulled)**
- **4 cups low-sodium beef broth**
- **1 cup water**
- **1 cup diced tomatoes (no salt added)**
- **1 teaspoon dried thyme**
- **1 teaspoon dried rosemary**
- **1 bay leaf**
- **Salt and pepper, to taste**
- **1 cup fresh parsley, chopped (for garnish)**
- **1 tablespoon fresh thyme (optional, for garnish)**

Procedures of Preparation

1. **Heat the Oil:**
   - In a large pot or Dutch oven, heat the olive oil over medium heat.
2. **Brown the Beef:**
   - Add the beef stew meat and cook until browned on all sides, about 7-10 minutes. Remove the beef and set aside.
3. **Sauté Vegetables:**
   - In the same pot, add the onion and garlic. Sauté the

onion for 5 minutes, or until soft. Cook for an additional 5 minutes after adding the carrots and celery.

4. **Add Barley and Liquid:**
    - Stir in the barley, beef broth, water, and diced tomatoes. Put the browned meat back into the pot.
5. **Season and Simmer:**
    - Pour in the dried thyme, rosemary, bay leaf, salt, and pepper. Stir thoroughly and bring to a boil.
6. **Cook the Soup:**
    - Reduce the heat to low, cover, and simmer for 50-60 minutes, or until the beef is tender and the barley is cooked through.
7. **Garnish and Serve:**
    - Remove the bay leaf. Garnish with fresh parsley and thyme, if using. Serve hot.

Nutritional Values (Per Serving)

- **Calories:** 300
- **Protein:** 20g
- **Carbohydrates:** 30g
- **Fat:** 10g
- **Fiber:** 6g
- **Sugar:** 6g
- **Potassium:** 600mg

Note: Nutritional values are approximate and can differ based on specific ingredients and quantities used.

Cooking Tips

- **Brown the Meat Well:** Browning the beef adds a rich flavor to the soup, enhancing its overall taste.
- **Adjust Barley:** If you prefer a thicker soup, increase the amount of barley slightly.
- **Fresh Herbs:** Adding fresh herbs at the end of cooking or as a garnish boosts the flavor and freshness of the soup.
- **Leftovers:** This soup stores well in the refrigerator for up to three days and freezes for up to three months. Reheat gently to avoid overcooking the barley.

Health Benefits

- **Protein-Rich:** Beef provides high-quality protein essential for muscle repair and overall health.
- **Barley Benefits:** Barley is a good source of fiber, which aids in digestion and supports heart health.
- **Nutrient-Dense:** The variety of vegetables adds important vitamins and minerals to the soup.

- **Hydrating:** With a high liquid content, this soup helps maintain hydration levels.
- **Heart-Healthy:** Using olive oil and lean beef contributes to a heart-healthy diet.

40. Butternut Squash Soup with Nutmeg

Preparation Time

- 15 minutes

Cooking Time

- 40 minutes

Serving Unit

- 6 servings

Ingredients

- 1 large butternut squash, peeled, seeded, and cubed (about 4 cups)
- 1 large onion, diced
- 2 cloves garlic, minced
- 2 tablespoons olive oil
- 4 cups low-sodium vegetable broth
- 1 cup water
- 1/2 teaspoon ground nutmeg
- 1/2 teaspoon ground cinnamon
- 1/2 teaspoon dried thyme
- Salt and pepper, to taste
- 1/4 cup heavy cream or coconut milk (optional for creaminess)
- Fresh parsley, chopped (for garnish, optional)

Procedures of Preparation

1. **Prepare the Squash:**
   - Peel, seed, and cube the butternut squash. Set aside.
2. **Sauté Aromatics:**
   - In a large pot, heat the olive oil over medium heat. Sauté the onion and garlic until the onion is transparent, about 5 minutes.
3. **Cook the Squash:**
   - Add the cubed butternut squash to the pot. Cook for about 5 minutes, stirring periodically.

4. **Add Liquid and Seasonings:**
   - Pour in the vegetable broth and water. Stir in the nutmeg, cinnamon, thyme, salt, and pepper. Bring to a boil.
5. **Simmer:**
   - Reduce the heat and let the soup simmer for 25-30 minutes, or until the butternut squash is tender.
6. **Blend the Soup:**
   - Puree the soup until smooth using an immersion blender. Alternatively, gently transfer the soup in stages to a blender.
7. **Add Cream (Optional):**
   - Stir in the heavy cream or coconut milk if desired for extra creaminess.
8. **Garnish and Serve:**
   - Garnish with fresh parsley if desired. Serve hot.

Nutritional Values (Per Serving)

- **Calories:** 150
- **Protein:** 2g
- **Carbohydrates:** 30g
- **Fat:** 4g
- **Fiber:** 5g
- **Sugar:** 8g
- **Potassium:** 600mg

Note: Nutritional values are approximate and can differ based on specific ingredients and quantities used.

Cooking Tips

- **Even Cooking:** Cut the butternut squash into uniform pieces to ensure even cooking and blending.
- **Adjust Spices:** Modify the amount of nutmeg and cinnamon to suit your taste preferences.
- **Cream Alternative:** For a dairy-free version, use coconut milk or almond milk.
- **Blender Caution:** If using a traditional blender, allow the soup to cool slightly before blending to avoid splatters.

Health Benefits

- **Rich in Vitamins:** Butternut squash is high in vitamins A and C, which are beneficial for vision and immune health.
- **Antioxidants:** Nutmeg and cinnamon provide antioxidants that can help reduce inflammation.
- **Digestive Health:** High fiber content supports digestive health and regularity.
- **Low in Calories:** This soup is low in calories and fat, making it a heart-healthy choice.
- **Versatile:** Can be adjusted for different dietary needs, including dairy-free options

28-Day Meal Plan

Introduction to Meal Planning

Meal planning is the process of organizing and preparing your meals in advance to ensure that your dietary needs and preferences are met consistently. For individuals managing health conditions like kidney disease, meal planning is especially important as it helps in controlling nutrient intake, such as sodium, potassium, and phosphorus, which are crucial for maintaining kidney health.

Planning meals ahead of time allows you to:

- **Ensure Nutritional Balance:** Tailor your meals to include the right balance of proteins, carbohydrates, fats, and essential nutrients.
- **Save Time and Stress:** Reduce daily decision-making and streamline your grocery shopping by knowing exactly what you'll need for the week.
- **Support Dietary Goals:** Stay on track with your health goals by sticking to a planned menu that aligns with your dietary restrictions and preferences.
- **Avoid Last-Minute Choices:** Prevent impulsive eating or reliance on less healthy, convenient foods by having ready-to-go meals.

Meal planning not only supports your health but also adds convenience and consistency to your daily routine, making it easier to maintain a balanced and nutritious diet.

28-Day Kidney-Friendly Meal Plan

Week 1

Day 1:

- **Breakfast:** Scrambled Egg Whites with Spinach
- **Lunch:** Turkey and Avocado Wraps
- **Dinner:** Baked Cod with Steamed Broccoli
- **Snacks:** Greek Yogurt with Fresh Berries, Apple Slices with Almond Butter

Day 2:

- **Breakfast:** Quinoa Porridge with Blueberries
- **Lunch:** Roasted Vegetable Soup
- **Dinner:** Sweet Potato and Lentil Stew
- **Snacks:** Cottage Cheese with Pineapple, Carrot Sticks with Hummus

Day 3:

- **Breakfast:** Low-Sodium Oatmeal with Almonds

- **Lunch:** Quinoa and Black Bean Salad
- **Dinner:** Herb-Crusted Salmon with Asparagus
- **Snacks:** Banana Smoothie with Flaxseed, Mixed Nuts and Dried Fruits

Day 4:

- **Breakfast:** Greek Yogurt with Fresh Berries
- **Lunch:** Spinach and Mushroom Frittata
- **Dinner:** Turkey Meatballs with Zucchini Noodles
- **Snacks:** Rice Cakes with Avocado, Cottage Cheese with Cucumber

Day 5:

- **Breakfast:** Chia Seed Pudding with Apple
- **Lunch:** Grilled Chicken Salad with Lemon Vinaigrette
- **Dinner:** Baked Chicken Breasts with Cauliflower Rice
- **Snacks:** Edamame Beans with Sea Salt, Fresh Fruit Salad with Mint

Day 6:

- **Breakfast:** Banana Smoothie with Flaxseed
- **Lunch:** Roasted Vegetable Soup
- **Dinner:** Beef Stir-Fry with Bell Peppers
- **Snacks:** Yogurt Parfait with Honey, Apple Slices with Almond Butter

Day 7:

- **Breakfast:** Cottage Cheese with Pineapple
- **Lunch:** Turkey and Avocado Wraps
- **Dinner:** Butternut Squash Soup with Nutmeg
- **Snacks:** Carrot Sticks with Hummus, Rice Cakes with Avocado

---

Week 2

Day 8:

- **Breakfast:** Quinoa Porridge with Blueberries
- **Lunch:** Spinach and Mushroom Frittata
- **Dinner:** Lemon Garlic Shrimp with Green Beans
- **Snacks:** Greek Yogurt with Fresh Berries, Mixed Nuts and Dried Fruits

Day 9:

- **Breakfast:** Low-Sodium Oatmeal with Almonds
- **Lunch:** Quinoa and Black Bean Salad
- **Dinner:** Baked Cod with Steamed Broccoli
- **Snacks:** Banana Smoothie with Flaxseed, Cottage Cheese with Cucumber

Day 10:

- **Breakfast:** Chia Seed Pudding with Apple
- **Lunch:** Grilled Chicken Salad with Lemon Vinaigrette
- **Dinner:** Sweet Potato and Lentil Stew
- **Snacks:** Edamame Beans with Sea Salt, Fresh Fruit Salad with Mint

Day 11:

- **Breakfast:** Greek Yogurt with Fresh Berries
- **Lunch:** Roasted Vegetable Soup
- **Dinner:** Herb-Crusted Salmon with Asparagus
- **Snacks:** Rice Cakes with Avocado, Mixed Nuts and Dried Fruits

Day 12:

- **Breakfast:** Scrambled Egg Whites with Spinach
- **Lunch:** Turkey Meatballs with Zucchini Noodles
- **Dinner:** Beef Stir-Fry with Bell Peppers
- **Snacks:** Cottage Cheese with Pineapple, Carrot Sticks with Hummus

Day 13:

- **Breakfast:** Low-Sodium Oatmeal with Almonds
- **Lunch:** Quinoa and Black Bean Salad
- **Dinner:** Baked Chicken Breasts with Cauliflower Rice
- **Snacks:** Yogurt Parfait with Honey, Apple Slices with Almond Butter

Day 14:

- **Breakfast:** Chia Seed Pudding with Apple
- **Lunch:** Spinach and Mushroom Frittata
- **Dinner:** Butternut Squash Soup with Nutmeg
- **Snacks:** Rice Cakes with Avocado, Edamame Beans with Sea Salt

---

Week 3

Day 15:

- **Breakfast:** Banana Smoothie with Flaxseed
- **Lunch:** Grilled Chicken Salad with Lemon Vinaigrette
- **Dinner:** Turkey Meatballs with Zucchini Noodles
- **Snacks:** Greek Yogurt with Fresh Berries, Mixed Nuts and Dried Fruits

Day 16:

- **Breakfast:** Greek Yogurt with Fresh Berries
- **Lunch:** Roasted Vegetable Soup
- **Dinner:** Lemon Garlic Shrimp with Green Beans
- **Snacks:** Cottage Cheese with Pineapple, Fresh Fruit Salad with Mint

Day 17:

- **Breakfast:** Quinoa Porridge with Blueberries
- **Lunch:** Spinach and Mushroom Frittata
- **Dinner:** Baked Cod with Steamed Broccoli
- **Snacks:** Apple Slices with Almond Butter, Rice Cakes with Avocado

Day 18:

- **Breakfast:** Scrambled Egg Whites with Spinach
- **Lunch:** Quinoa and Black Bean Salad
- **Dinner:** Sweet Potato and Lentil Stew
- **Snacks:** Edamame Beans with Sea Salt, Yogurt Parfait with Honey

Day 19:

- **Breakfast:** Low-Sodium Oatmeal with Almonds
- **Lunch:** Grilled Chicken Salad with Lemon Vinaigrette
- **Dinner:** Beef Stir-Fry with Bell Peppers
- **Snacks:** Banana Smoothie with Flaxseed, Carrot Sticks with Hummus

Day 20:

- **Breakfast:** Chia Seed Pudding with Apple
- **Lunch:** Turkey and Avocado Wraps
- **Dinner:** Baked Chicken Breasts with Cauliflower Rice
- **Snacks:** Mixed Nuts and Dried Fruits, Cottage Cheese with Cucumber

Day 21:

- **Breakfast:** Greek Yogurt with Fresh Berries
- **Lunch:** Roasted Vegetable Soup
- **Dinner:** Herb-Crusted Salmon with Asparagus
- **Snacks:** Apple Slices with Almond Butter, Fresh Fruit Salad with Mint

---

Week 4

Day 22:

- **Breakfast:** Scrambled Egg Whites with Spinach
- **Lunch:** Turkey Meatballs with Zucchini Noodles
- **Dinner:** Lemon Garlic Shrimp with Green Beans
- **Snacks:** Rice Cakes with Avocado, Mixed Nuts and Dried Fruits

Day 23:

- **Breakfast:** Quinoa Porridge with Blueberries
- **Lunch:** Spinach and Mushroom Frittata
- **Dinner:** Beef Stir-Fry with Bell Peppers

- **Snacks:** Greek Yogurt with Fresh Berries, Carrot Sticks with Hummus

Day 24:

- **Breakfast:** Low-Sodium Oatmeal with Almonds
- **Lunch:** Grilled Chicken Salad with Lemon Vinaigrette
- **Dinner:** Sweet Potato and Lentil Stew
- **Snacks:** Edamame Beans with Sea Salt, Banana Smoothie with Flaxseed

Day 25:

- **Breakfast:** Chia Seed Pudding with Apple
- **Lunch:** Roasted Vegetable Soup
- **Dinner:** Baked Cod with Steamed Broccoli
- **Snacks:** Cottage Cheese with Pineapple, Fresh Fruit Salad with Mint

Day 26:

- **Breakfast:** Greek Yogurt with Fresh Berries
- **Lunch:** Quinoa and Black Bean Salad
- **Dinner:** Butternut Squash Soup with Nutmeg
- **Snacks:** Rice Cakes with Avocado, Mixed Nuts and Dried Fruits

Day 27:

- **Breakfast:** Scrambled Egg Whites with Spinach
- **Lunch:** Turkey and Avocado Wraps
- **Dinner:** Baked Chicken Breasts with Cauliflower Rice
- **Snacks:** Apple Slices with Almond Butter, Edamame Beans with Sea Salt

Day 28:

- **Breakfast:** Low-Sodium Oatmeal with Almonds
- **Lunch:** Spinach and Mushroom Frittata
- **Dinner:** Lemon Garlic Shrimp with Green Beans
- **Snacks:** Yogurt Parfait with Honey, Carrot Sticks with Hummus

Printable Shopping List

Fruits & Vegetables

- Apples (for slices and chia pudding)
- Blueberries (for porridge and parfait)
- Bananas (for smoothies)
- Pineapple (for cottage cheese)
- Fresh berries (for yogurt and parfait)
- Spinach (for scrambled egg whites and frittata)
- Broccoli (for steaming)
- Sweet potatoes (for stew)
- Zucchini (for noodles)
- Asparagus (for salmon)
- Green beans (for shrimp)
- Carrots (for sticks)
- Bell peppers (for stir-fry)
- Butternut squash (for soup and risotto)
- Cucumbers (for cottage cheese)
- Avocados (for wraps and rice cakes)
- Fresh mint (for fruit salad)
- Lemons (for vinaigrette and shrimp)
- Garlic (for shrimp and soup)
- Mushrooms (for frittata)
- Onions (for various recipes)
- Tomatoes (for soup)

Proteins

- Egg whites (for scrambled eggs)
- Greek yogurt (for breakfast and parfait)
- Turkey breast (for meatballs and wraps)
- Cod (for baking)
- Chicken breasts (for baking and salad)
- Salmon (for baking)
- Shrimp (for grilling)
- Beef (for stir-fry)
- Cottage cheese (for snacks)
- Lentils (for stew and soup)
- Black beans (for salad)

Grains & Cereals

- Quinoa (for porridge and salad)
- Oatmeal (for breakfast)
- Brown rice (for stuffed peppers)
- Barley (for soup)
- Rice cakes (for snacks)

Dairy & Alternatives

- Almond milk (if needed for oatmeal or other recipes)

Nuts & Seeds

- Almonds (for oatmeal and snacks)
- Flaxseed (for smoothies)
- Chia seeds (for pudding)
- Mixed nuts (for snacks)

Condiments & Spices

- Olive oil (for cooking and salad dressing)
- Honey (for yogurt parfait)
- Sea salt (for seasoning)
- Cinnamon (for apples and recipes)
- Nutmeg (for soup)
- Black pepper (for seasoning)

- Fresh herbs (like basil and parsley for soups)

Other Essentials

- Hummus (for carrot sticks)
- Almond butter (for apple slices)
- Fresh herbs (for soups and salads)

Tips for Shopping:

- Check your pantry and refrigerator to see if you already have some of these items.
- Buy fresh produce weekly for the best quality.
- For long shelf-life items like grains, nuts, and canned goods, you can stock up in bulk.

Feel free to adjust the quantities based on your needs and preferences. Happy shopping!

Conclusion

Embracing a Kidney-Friendly Lifestyle

Adopting a kidney-friendly lifestyle is not just about making dietary changes—it's about embracing a new way of living that prioritizes your health and well-being. For those undergoing dialysis or managing kidney concerns, the right diet plays a crucial role in maintaining overall health and improving quality of life. This journey involves making informed choices that align with your health needs, and your commitment to this lifestyle can significantly impact your health outcomes.

A kidney-friendly lifestyle focuses on reducing the intake of substances that can strain the kidneys, such as sodium, potassium, and phosphorus, while ensuring you get the nutrients necessary to support your body. It also involves balancing fluid intake and managing protein consumption. Embracing this lifestyle means understanding how different foods affect your body and making choices that help manage and potentially improve kidney function.

By incorporating recipes that are specifically designed to be low in sodium, potassium, and phosphorus, you can better manage your kidney health while still enjoying flavorful and satisfying meals. The recipes in this book are crafted to help you enjoy a variety of dishes that adhere to dietary guidelines while also appealing to your taste buds.

Tips for Success on Dialysis

1. **Plan Your Meals**: Planning ahead is essential. Use the meal plans and recipes provided to create a structured eating schedule. This helps ensure you consistently follow your dietary guidelines and reduces the likelihood of impulsive, less nutritious food choices.
2. **Monitor Portion Sizes**: Pay close attention to portion sizes to avoid overeating or consuming excess nutrients that could strain your kidneys. Measuring your food can help maintain portion control and ensure you stay within your dietary limits.
3. **Stay Hydrated**: While managing fluid intake is crucial, it’s also important to stay hydrated. Work with your healthcare provider to determine the right amount of fluid for your individual needs. Consuming water-rich, kidney-friendly foods can help meet hydration needs without excessive fluid intake.
4. **Read Labels Carefully**: When shopping for groceries, always read food labels to check for sodium, potassium, and phosphorus content. Avoid

processed foods that are high in these nutrients, and choose fresh, whole foods whenever possible.

5. **Experiment with Flavors**: One of the challenges of a kidney-friendly diet can be the perceived lack of flavor. Try different herbs and spices to improve taste without increasing sodium. Fresh herbs like basil, cilantro, and parsley can make a big difference in enhancing the taste of your dishes.
6. **Consult with a Dietitian**: Regular consultations with a dietitian who specializes in kidney health can provide personalized advice and adjustments to your diet as needed. They can help you navigate challenges and ensure you're meeting your nutritional needs effectively.
7. **Stay Active**: Alongside dietary changes, maintaining an active lifestyle is beneficial. Exercise can help manage weight, improve overall health, and enhance your quality of life. Aim for regular, moderate activity that fits your health status and lifestyle.

Encouragement for Your Culinary Journey

Embarking on a culinary journey with a focus on kidney health can be both rewarding and empowering. It's a chance to explore new flavors, discover nutritious ingredients, and create meals that support your well-being. Embrace the opportunity to experiment with recipes, try new cooking techniques, and find joy in the kitchen.

Remember, this journey is about progress, not perfection. There will be challenges, but each step you take towards healthier eating is a victory. Celebrate the small successes, whether it's mastering a new recipe or simply making a healthier choice. Your efforts in the kitchen are a crucial part of your overall health strategy, and every positive change contributes to better managing your condition.

Stay motivated by focusing on the benefits of a kidney-friendly diet—improved energy levels, better management of your condition, and an enhanced quality of life. As you continue to cook and eat with intention, you'll find that this journey not only supports your kidney health but also enriches your life with new culinary experiences.

Your commitment to a kidney-friendly lifestyle is a powerful step towards better health. Embrace the journey with enthusiasm and optimism, knowing that each meal you prepare brings you closer to achieving your health goals and living a fulfilling life.

Made in the USA
Las Vegas, NV
29 January 2025

17178879R00083